SEEN LOCALLY

Henry Pluckrose

ROUTLEDGE
London

First published in 1989 by
Routledge
11 New Fetter Lane, London EC4P 4EE

© 1989 Henry Pluckrose

Filmset by Mayhew Typesetting, Bristol, England
Printed and bound in Great Britain by
Biddles Ltd, Guildford and King's Lynn

British Library Cataloguing in Publication Data

Pluckrose, Henry, 1931–
    Seen locally.
    1. Education. Curriculum subjects.
    Environmental studies – Bibliographies
    I. Title
    330.7'07

ISBN 0–415–01603–7

Contents

Foreword

This book will provide a supportive companion for any teacher planning to make use of the wider environment outside the classroom. The idea of taking children out into the real world is now commonplace yet, until now, little training or advice has been available for what is one of the most demanding – and rewarding – forms of education.

Not that the desire to explore, understand, and enjoy the world is new: the school visit is part of a long and rich tradition. It is part of the civilizing process. Provincials from the outer reaches of the empire flocked to Rome to wonder at (and later copy) the great buildings and sophisticated ways of their masters.

In the 18th century young men made the Grand Tour of Europe, and some seem to have been at least as badly behaved as modern hooligans, but the majority came home cultivated gentlemen, laden with new ideas and the booty which now enriches the very houses and museums to which we bring our children.

At best these cultural pilgrims were well prepared by their often distinguished tutors, so they were able to appreciate the significance of classical allusions, they had a 'grammar' to help them judge a landscape, and they had been trained to be reasonably accomplished artists and musicians before they set out on their travels.

Henry Pluckrose has rightly emphasized the importance of relating environmental exploration to the arts. Until we destroy their sensitivity, as too frequently parents and, sometimes, teachers do through lack of technique or brusque demands to 'hurry along' and 'stop wasting time', children are prepared to explore this wonderful and strange world with every sense alert. We must never forget that every visit should be an infinitely precious new experience to the children, who are at least as sensitive to the attitude of the adult accompanying them as to the place itself. We must tread softly, because we tread on their dreams.

John Hodgson
Education Adviser, National Trust

Acknowledgements

I should like to record my thanks to the people who have helped me in the presentation of this book: Bridget Jackson, for her line drawings; Brigid Bell, of Routledge, for her advice during the initial discussions of the manuscript; and Roz Sullivan, for the care she has shown in preparing the typescript.

Finally, I should thank all the children I have worked with who have led me to believe by the enthusiasm they have shown for such things as cadavers and dungeons, water-mills, and lighthouses, that this book will be of some use to all who work with young children.

1 Introduction

Children acquire information and learn to respond imaginatively to
what they see, hear and otherwise experience. (*Primary Education in
England*, HMSO, 1978)

Over the past thirty-five years I have devoted much of my time to
inviting children and student teachers to look, to see, and to reflect
upon the images their eyes receive. With children, the task has been
comparatively easy. Children's curiosity – like that of Kipling's
Elephant-child – seems to be insatiable; their experiences of life being
limited, they explore the world through their senses. Each new
encounter expands understanding and provides a foundation for
future learning.

The adults with whom I have worked have often found the
challenge more difficult to meet. Perhaps this is because they have
learned how to live with images which require but a fleeting glance
– the trite advertisement, the flashing neon sign, and the 'new' shop-
ping centre whose only noteworthy characteristic is that it looks and
feels exactly the same as every other in the land. Certainly older eyes
seem to have become jaded, blinded by the sameness to everyday
existence.

The causes of this are rooted in the past. Today's adults were of
course once children. The great majority of them sent to schools,
which at best ignored and at worst denied, the significance and
importance of visual literacy.

The consequences of this neglect have been profound. Human
beings do not learn only from books and the spoken word. They

learn best by being immersed in experience which calls for a response from their whole being, which fires the imagination, and triggers off a desire to discover more. Those of us who work with young children – shaped by our own past – will need to learn new skills if we are to help the next generation to become visually aware. Somehow we must give our own senses, emotions, and imagination more time to respond to the environment in which we find ourselves. Then, and only then, will we begin to appreciate how vital it is for us to give the same opportunity to the children in our care.

Some years ago I was working with a group of teachers in a Folk Museum in Lund, a medieval university city in southern Sweden. One of the group, a lady in her late fifties, became so fascinated with the decoration on some fifteenth-century pottery that she had no time to study any other exhibit. The drawings and notes she made, rich in detail, filled several pages of her sketch-book. Her final comments remain with me: 'I've been here so many times but never paused to look. Why has it taken me fifty years to see? Why have I been so keen to make my children hurry?'

Fortunately this book has been written against a background of change. Teachers no longer regard learning simply within the context of textbooks and classrooms. Children, at a very early stage in their school life *are* being helped to relate book-learning to the real world, and much creative work is built upon a marriage of imagination and actual experience.

And yet, although children are no longer 'anchored' to their desks as they were in my childhood, the curriculum in too many of our schools (we need only turn to the published reports of Her Majesty's Inspectorate for evidence) remains somewhat circumscribed. All too often subjects remain isolated and the cross-curriculum links which give meaning and purpose to the learning tend to be ignored. It seems to me that although progress has been made, our perception remains that of Mr Polly: 'It's only school that turns the young child from someone who wonders at the marvels around him into someone who sees them only in terms of History and Geography.'

The need to move towards a curriculum in which the subjects are seen as complementary parts of a unified whole has been long in coming. As the Newsom Report in 1963 observed, 'The separate lessons and subjects are single pieces of a mosaic: what matters most is not the numbers and colours of the separate pieces but what pattern they make when put together'.*

An integrated curriculum must be set within the context of fundamental changes in contemporary life. We live in an age

Half our Future, London: HMSO, 1963, para. 83, p. 29.

dominated by the micro-chip, and of world-wide, immediate mass communication. Children whose approach to understanding has been shaped from birth by dramatic, moving visual images conveyed into their home by TV screens are unlikely to respond enthusiastically to a school programme which ignores the reality of the world beyond the school walls. Television has been accused, with some justification, of turning children into passive 'lookers on'. However, it has also resulted in children being far better informed on a wide range of issues, more sophisticated in their demands, and less willing to respond to information presented in a drab and lifeless manner.

Once we accept that technological advances have in some ways made the teacher's task more difficult, it becomes obvious that those of us who work with young children need to rethink the ways in which knowledge is presented to them. Information, appropriately filleted to reflect our understanding of the age and ability of the children in our care, and imparted in installments, may be all that children require to pass a test or meet a curriculum target. Unfortunately the mastery of such filleted information will do little to make them effective *learners*, induce a thirst to seek out further information for its own sake, or encourage them to regard learning as a positive activity in which each individual participates actively and personally. Passivity, once the measure of a well-run class, is unlikely to create an enthusiasm for learning which is taken from childhood into adulthood. Thus I would suggest that an education programme which makes demands of the learner within his or her own environment is likely to be more effective than one which is based upon abstractions.

Such a programme makes more demands upon the teacher than the traditional textbook approach. Children, when confronted with, say, an *actual* Norman keep or a *live* swan turning her eggs, will invariably ask questions of subtlety and challenge. Each child's perceptions and interests, being personal, provoke an idiosyncratic response to the experience. The child is therefore quite unlike the writer of textbooks, whose skill is measured by ability to package information.

Children do not acquire information in a finite form, nor do they necessarily retain the information which we would have them master. The task of the teacher is therefore to develop as far as possible a learning programme which will encourage the mastery of research, recording, and presentation skills appropriate to each child. Of course, such an approach creates some problems. Not all children will master the same facts, fill the same number of pages, or be interested in the same things. Fortunately the quantity of facts remembered is not the mark of an educated mind. Learning is as much about process as it is about product. The person – be he/she young or old – who has learned *how to find out* is much more likely to be able to discover the information he or she needs for a particular purpose than the person who has been drilled into the acquisition of facts for no perceptible purpose.

This book has been written to indicate ways in which close observation of place can provide the starting-point of a learning programme, and to show how information which the adult and child obtain together can be recorded through pictures, models, maps, plans, and photographs as well as the written and spoken word. As with all books on environmental studies, the biggest difficulty which has to be overcome is in presenting ideas so as to make them meaningful to teachers working in different parts of the country. The teacher working in a decaying inner city has, at first glance, far less to draw upon than the teacher whose school is located in, say, Chester; similarly, the teacher in, say, Caernarfon would seem to be blessed with far richer evidence of the past than a colleague teaching in a tiny school in a remote Welsh valley.

And yet wherever people have lived, they have altered and shaped their environment. The houses and flats in which children live, the roads and pathways which criss-cross their neighbourhood, the local shop, and the weed-covered railway track, and the school itself, all throw light upon past and present. Each element comments upon the struggle of men and women to master the physical world – to cut down trees, clear and drain the land; to grow crops; to quarry stone and build; to dig, shape, and fire clay; to extract metals; to fashion straw, reed, and willow; and to use materials to construct places in which to live securely.

This, then, is a book of suggestions, which can be drawn upon to give depth and dimension to local studies. My concentration on the ways in which beings have shaped and altered their environment by building, and often by draining and reclaiming land in so doing, is deliberate. I have made no attempt to feature the world of nature, an aspect of environmental studies which merits a volume of its own. Let me observe, however, that children with whom I have worked have visited many castles and monasteries and left the site richer in their understanding of birds and wild flowers than when they entered. The effective teacher never frustrates children's desire to learn by forcing them to conform to studies so narrowly based that the joy and excitement which comes from seeing something for the first time (a flower in a castle wall or parent birds feeding their young in a nest in a ruined window) is dismissed as irrelevant because this new interest does not comfortably fit with the topic being considered.

Finally, I should stress that the aim and purpose of this book is simply to provide teachers with a starting-point for local research. It has been prepared as a source book of ideas which can be developed and extended within the curriculum guidelines of each school. The activities suggested are not related to age or to ability; each child can walk through a village, amble down a street, explore a lighthouse, farmhouse, or harbour, and draw upon this experience at his or her own level. What is important is that each successive experience is used to develop enquiry and understanding and that the essential skills of recording and research will be deepened in the process. *Environmental enquiry*, which is the term I use to describe the approach outlined in this book, succeeds because each child can become a detective, a researcher: each pair of eyes represents an individual and personal viewpoint which can be expressed in the drawn line or written and spoken word.

Before preparing this introduction, I happened to glance through some work which followed on a visit made by a group of 9-year-olds to Smithfield meat market. They had gone there to look at the ways in which the Victorians had used iron and glass, in order to be better able to compare the construction of the market hall with that of a nearby railway station. Among the work produced were architectural drawings, descriptions of the work of meat porters, and sketches of animal carcasses being prepared for the kitchen, and there was also some writing about iron and glass. What stands out above all, however, is a short poem; I include it here because it indicates the quality of response which we can expect when children are touched by the atmosphere of place:

> Its like the devils house
> Meat hanging in wardrobes
> Like bloody dresses to wear.

When children are really encouraged to look at their environment, they will begin to see. Responses will not always be the commonplace or the expected. What is important is that we are sensitive to the children's individual responses, using them to give point and purpose to learning.

2 Approaches to local study

We live in a country that is richer than any other in the visible remains of the past but . . . most of us are visually illiterate. (W. G. Hoskins, *Fieldwork in Local History*, 1967)

Nowadays there can be few schools whose curriculum is centred entirely upon the classroom, upon explanations given by teachers, and books. Indeed it could be said that the most significant development in educational methodology of recent years has been the realization that young children learn most effectively when their learning is based upon first-hand experience. That children learn best when they are encouraged to become totally immersed in a subject merits little comment here. Throughout the year museums, castles, harbours, hill forts, streets, markets, and churches are exploited by teachers as starting-points for children's learning.

The use of the everyday environment not only serves to vivify learning. It also enables every child to draw heavily upon their senses. Learning becomes more than sitting still and being drenched with words. It becomes an activity in which listening is enriched with touching, smelling, seeing, and perhaps even tasting. Inevitably such emersion of the senses evokes a personal response, heightening sensitivity and deepening understanding and awareness.

This heightened sensitivity is reflected in both the quality of children's written and spoken responses. It is also reflected in their sensitivity to place. 'I can almost *feel* the monks singing', one 9-year-old said to me as we stood in a floodlit Fountains Abbey: 'I could easily believe in God if I spent all my life here.'

Taking children out of the classroom is one way of deepening and confirming book-learning. Using the world beyond the classroom as the starting-point for study has encouraged teachers to rethink their approach to curriculum development.

Children do not compartmentalize their experiences (be these experiences in school or out of it) into tightly bound subject areas: science and history, geography and mathematics, English and computer studies, art and music, moral education, and environmental studies all overlap and intertwine. When we present Tudor England to a group of 10-year-olds, can we do so without touching upon the dress, music, customs, religious beliefs, and methods of building of the period? Can a study of the Tudors make anything but the most superficial sense to children unless we, the teachers, make some attempt to explain the Tudor World and the ideas which underpinned it? Similarly, a group of 5- and 6-year-olds using the local market as the centre-point of a topic are bound to confront mathematics (mapping and graphing, e.g. number and type of shops or stalls), art and craft (picture-making and modelling), and language (oral work during and after a visit and written work following upon it) as well as environmental issues ('Why is the market there?' 'Was there a market in the square when my mother or grandmother was a child?' 'Who runs the market?' 'Who clears up the refuse and why?').

An approach to learning which is as broadly based as this tends to ignore subject boundaries. This is not to suggest that the skills which underpin particular academic disciplines are forgotten. Children will need to be helped to appreciate concepts which are fundamental to the understanding of science, history, geography, and mathematics.

The need to widen and deepen the programme which is offered to young children has been stressed in the curriculum guidelines prepared by Her Majesty's Inspectorate. In each of them cross-curriculum approaches are commended. It is appropriate that they should be.

We have already noted that it is difficult to compartmentalize school subjects. It is even more difficult for young children to work within the restraints of a formal academic discipline. Children tend to respond to the new situations in which they find themselves with an immediacy which can throw awry the best laid of plans. A visit to a post-mill is likely to be remembered as much for the dog which lay across the door when the children entered the building as for the fact that the millstones came from France.

Taking children out of school as a means of confirming and clarifying information obtained within the classroom deepens understanding. It encourages them to look, to see, and question, and also to set newly acquired knowledge within a contextual framework:

Ways of looking (1): looking for differences. How do these two ceilings differ? How does this window differ from those found in a modern home?

'Charles II was a tall man. And he hid in a priest-hole as small at that!' The 8-year-old visiting Boscobel House (Shropshire) paused for a moment and then observed, 'He must really have been frightened of capture'.

For a learning programme to be effective it should allow each child to bring his or her own interests and perceptions to it. Inevitably this will mean that any programme which we design as teachers will produce a somewhat uneven response. Since it is this unevenness which so often causes concern, let me now consider some strategies which allow children to be challenged at a personal level and, at the same time, provide teachers with a secure framework within which to work.

It is obvious that out-of-school activities require careful, specific preparation. But first an obvious question needs to be asked: what will this experience give to my class? There must be a sound educational reason for every school visit. It follows therefore that those taking part will gain information which is particular to the experience. For example, it seems pointless to me to take children to the ruin of a medieval abbey, so that while they are there, they should be invited to copy a drawing of a monk from a wall display in the Chapter House. Such an activity diverts children from the real purpose of the visit: to explore *at first hand* evidence of the past.

Ways of looking: (2): looking for similarities. This is a picture
of a castle stairway. Where might a newel staircase be found
in a contemporary building?

Ways of looking (3): comparisons. How does this range compare with that used
in the school kitchen? In which ways does it comment upon life-style in the
past?

Ways of looking (4): looking for detail. A study of pattern can be just as rewarding as a more broadly based study

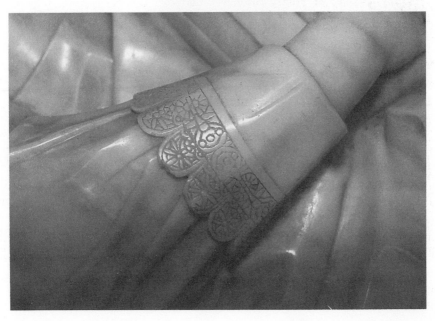

A study of ornament can be as significant as an analysis of architectural style. This carving of a man's face is to be found in Southall Minster. In legend he is known by many names: Puck, the Green Man, Robin Goodfellow, Robin Hood

Each visit will offer particular opportunities. Since it falls to the teacher to decide the direction which the children are to be encouraged to follow, it is helpful if the teacher knows the place which is being visited. Pre-visits are not only invaluable because they help focus upon the topics which could be studied by the children, but also promote self-confidence. To *know* where the toilets are situated after a long coach ride can be as important an element in the success of a trip as a bag full of sharpened pencils! Many centres (e.g. Beaulieu Abbey, in Hampshire; Yeoman's House, Wakefield; and a number of sites maintained by the National Trust) arrange 'teachers' days' on which teachers are encouraged to explore the site and to learn of the specialist provision which is offered to school parties.

Pre-visits give teachers the opportunity to collect material for classroom use – maps and posters for display; and pictures, postcards, and booklets for use in preparatory lessons. When it is impossible to make such a visit, information can often be obtained by post. Wherever appropriate, it is useful to collect material which illustrates the area being visited within the context of change over time. Old maps which illustrate how land has been engulfed by building (or how land, once used, is now neglected), and the growth and decay of an area as shown through contemporary prints, are invaluable ways of helping children grasp something of the paradox of continuity and change which is central to the understanding of history.

The great increase in recent years of the number of sites which welcome school parties (be these bird sanctuaries or open museums) has been accompanied by an explosion of printed material designed for children.

Ways of looking (5): looking at function. Why is this window so narrow? Does examination from the inside help us better to appreciate its design and construction?

In the majority of cases this printed material takes the form of an all-purpose worksheet. Sadly, the worksheet can quickly become the reason for the visit, its completion marking the end of the experience. Too often the questions themselves are closed (and thus from the teacher's standpoint conveniently markable), encouraging little reflection or self-questioning. Too often they direct the children's eyes to those things which the worksheet planner feels to be significant. In my experience children are much more likely to see if they are encouraged to look for themselves. Visual literacy cannot be taught through typed sheets of A4.

On a more fundamental level the 'closed' worksheet reduces the children's need to look at artefacts, for the answers almost invariably lie in the labelling. To ignore the source in order to concentrate upon an interpretation of it is unsound.

Dr Fines, of the West Sussex Institute of Higher Education, argues that worksheets, many of which prompt a 'Le Mans style start

Ways of looking (6): the unexpected. A door for the miller, a hole for his cat

followed by a race to the finish', demean the experience itself and reflect ill upon the respect we should show to children. For the less able they are disaster-ridden. 'Visits', he observes,

> help children to learn how to value. They are being asked not just to see something rare and special, but also to respond to the experience. Valuing is a high level skill. We should not exclude it from our educational aims simply because it is difficult.

If prepared material is to be offered to children – and throughout this book I include some possible prototypes – I would argue that it must be open-ended to allow each child the opportunity to comment upon the experience in an individual way and provide a starting-point for further research in the school or class library. Also in the chapters which follow I indicate approaches which serve to concentrate children's minds. For example, if a child knows that he/she will be invited to produce a map, an illustrated plan, a guidebook, a display of photographs, sketches, or line drawings, 'word pictures' of the people associated with the site, or a 'sound magazine' on tape, as a record of the visit, then the whole project begins with a focus. The challenge shapes the approach. If activities such as those listed above are shared between a group of children, the material collected will be wide-ranging and the corporate experience much fuller than would be the case had each child followed and completed an identical worksheet.

Pre-visits by teachers should also help to identify those adults associated with the site who might be prepared to talk to the children. Here I am not just thinking of the museum curator, the official guide, and the schools' officer, but also those people who have lived or worked in an area for many years, and who are able to comment upon the changes that have occurred in their lifetime.

The importance of oral history cannot be over-emphasized. A thatcher or a hedger telling of their boyhood experiences of their apprenticeship, and of the tools and equipment they use *are* living history. The very humanity of this situation, of the old talking to the young, bridges the years. Usually it is easier for craftsmen and women to talk to children in their own surroundings: one ladies' maid spoke at great length to a group of children in the garden of her almshouse, but she was tongue-tied in comparison when brought into school to talk.

In passing, it is worth remembering that the children's parents and grandparents can also be called upon to extend and deepen information collected on school visits. One parent with whom I worked – a transport worker – was an expert in the history of flight and the development of aircraft. Consequently he was much in demand whenever a visit to an aircraft museum was planned, both as a leader during the visit and as an accomplished model-maker afterwards.

As we have seen, a crucial aspect of any visit is *content* – and how this content should be presented. However, before commenting on how children might record their experiences, it is important to reflect upon how the impact of every school visit can be heightened by a sensitive use of time. Little is achieved if children regard out-of-school trips with distaste, born of being made to march crocodile-fashion around a museum, stately home, castle, or monastic ruin. Visits should fire the child's imagination, deepen understanding, and provide a stimulus for further work on return to school. Case upon case of exhibits, room after room of furniture, wall on wall of paintings, or pond on pond of wildfowl, do not of themselves stimulate – they tend to deaden. What we need to do, then, is to sharpen the impact of each visit by consciously restricting the time when children spend in any one place and being prepared to offer a range of activities. For example, it would be possible to take children to Ickworth House, in Suffolk, and spend several hours sketching or drawing inside it. If the activities within the house are balanced and

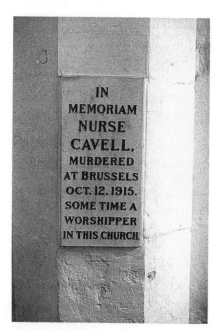

IN
MEMORIAM
NURSE
CAVELL,
MURDERED
AT BRUSSELS
OCT. 12. 1915.
SOME TIME A
WORSHIPPER
IN THIS CHURCH

EDITH CAVELL NURSE
PATRIOT AND MARTYR

Ways of looking (7): making
connections. This inscription (in
Steeple Bumpstead church, Essex)
indicates how local people felt
about the execution of an English
nurse in the First World War. In
Norwich a memorial commemorates
her bravery

supplemented by allowing the children to follow a nature trail and visit the deer park, the total experience is likely to be that much greater.

In my experience it is always more profitable to visit a site twice with a break of several weeks in between than to cram everything into one day. Over-stimulation, giving the children far too much material for them to assimilate, is short-sighted. It is possible to see so much that one ends up remembering nothing.

Pre-visits should therefore serve to indicate the kinds of activity which it is possible to undertake. Activity will be shaped and, to some extent, determined by the site itself. Visiting a popular museum in June might well restrict children to making small sketches; if this level of activity appears likely to be inappropriate for a particular group, it is often wiser to forgo the experience and use the time elsewhere.

When using a pre-visit to discover the most appropriate kinds of activity for the class to be taken to the site, one ingredient central to the experience is often forgotten: does this site offer any opportunity for the children to be quiet and enrich themselves in the atmosphere which it may generate. It is difficult to see such an opportunity arising in the bustle of York Minster at the height of the tourist season, but many sites do provide the opportunity for reflection: 6- and 7-year-olds taken from the city centre to the parklands of a country estate should be encouraged to listen to the sounds of nature; 10-year-olds standing, say, in the ruined chapel of Ludlow Castle should be encouraged to stand and imagine. All too often children are invited to write, draw, record, and be active; if they are to learn effectively, children (like us) need time to reflect. 'Have you thought', an 8-year-old said on reaching the top of the tower at Ely Cathedral, 'people built all of this without modern tools? And if it was as cold as this when they built it [it was snowing at the time], their hands must have been very sore.'

Obviously the part which school visits play in the overall programme of a school depends upon the approach to learning adopted by the headteacher and staff. The amount of time which is devoted to visits varies greatly from school to school and it would be inappropriate for me to suggest a model for all to follow. In passing, however, it is worth noting that the children's skills in recording in word and line, in using tape and film, and in making maps and developing their own simple survey sheets will only come with experience. With 5-year-olds, Environmental Studies may be little more than an exploration of the streets around the school, learning in the process how to look for the changing shapes of chimney-pots, windows, or doorways, and noting the variety of symbols, words, and colours which are used to give information to pedestrians and motorists. Such trips will, over time, help shape the children's view of learning. Exploring through the spoken word things seen and experienced provides the groundwork for writing.

Thus if children (and their parents) are encouraged to realize that learning is not simply desk bound and book based, and that the school visit is an integral part of the process of obtaining, recording, sifting, classifying and presenting information, then it is unlikely that 'taking children out' will be regarded either as a chore or as a termly or yearly 'treat'. Children are more likely to behave indifferently when they are ill-prepared for a new experience. By helping them to regard 'enquiry' as a natural vehicle for learning the local environment can be exploited. The skills and approaches learned locally can then be easily applied on more extended visits – both with the school and with parents.

There is another cogent reason for teaching enquiry skills with the area that children know well, for children need to have some understanding of the area in which they themselves live before they are taken long distances to study other communities. When the study is local, the children themselves have much to offer – from old family photographs to stories handed down from parents and grandparents.

Materials to support studies based upon the school's immediate area can be obtained from the municiple or county archivist (details obtainable through the local library or the town/county hall). These may include prints and drawings; photographs and postcards; transparencies; maps, plans, and surveyors' drawings; press cuttings and local newspapers; parish records; Poor Law records; the minutes and publications of local societies; and local directories.* Some local authorities have information available on microfiche, films, video tapes, and floppy discs.

In this connection 9- and 10-year-olds will find the school log-book of interest. If the school dates back to Victorian times, there will be much worth commenting on. Even if the school has been only recently opened, its name might well prompt research.

As knowledge of the immediate locality deepens, the distance which the children are taken from the school can be increased. Local studies – which may include work on such themes as churches, markets, street names and transport services – can be used to show the group how the knowledge acquired can be recorded as well as

---

* Most of these date from the nineteenth century, listing residents of an area – 'private' and 'commercial' – and clearly indicate the trades and professions followed. The best known is Kelly's Directory, other compilers include Kemp, Pigot, Robson, and Smith.

giving the children valuable experience on the use of reference books, maps, and local archives.

Every visit, be it within walking distance of the school or one which requires coach and train travel, must meet the requirements of the local education authority (LEA). Every authority has drawn up detailed guidelines – many of them carefully revised following the deaths of four children on a school trip to Land's End in 1985. The guidelines relate to such things as the age of the children and the ratio of supervising adults to the children, and the status of the adults involved (a parent is not, in every circumstance, regarded as the legal equivalent of a teacher); and they make recommendations as to the appropriateness of the activities undertaken. If an overnight stay is involved, some LEAs require assurance that the site has been visited prior to the trip and that it meets certain minimum requirements (e.g. that there are adequate washing and toilet facilities, and that the building meets the local authority health and safety regulations). Although membership of a professional association will give a modicum of protection against anything untoward happening on a visit, insurance is always advisable. The School Journey Association, 48 Cavendish Road, London SW12 (Tel. 01-675 2907) can advise on policies which are available and arrange appropriate cover.

Insurance costs money – as do entrance fees and fares. Education in the state sector is free, and schools cannot demand that parents contribute towards the cost of taking children out (though many parents are happy to do so). I therefore believe that the staff of each school should determine the place that environmental studies are to occupy in the curriculum. This may result in an agreed percentage of the capitation being set aside for visits or a special fund being opened for this purpose (perhaps supported by parent–teacher association (PTA) appeals and jumble sales).

This chapter is largely devoted to an examination of the teacher's role in developing an approach to children learning through environmental studies. One aspect which will not be touched upon in any great detail in the chapters which follow is the way in which the life and work of people who once lived in the area can be used as the starting-point for local studies.

Every town and many villages in the country boast a statue or two. Often these commemorate the life of local worthies who have some claim to fame, even if their names are not always included in school history books. Such statues often provide a fascinating starting-point for individual topic work: Who was this person? When did they live? What did they do? What can I find out about them in the library or county museum? I do not propose to provide a lengthy list, but the following examples will serve to illustrate my point: John Bunyan, the

Nonconformist writer, and John Howard, the prison reformer (Bedford); Alfred the Great (Wantage); John Hampden, of Ship Money fame (Aylesbury); Richard Trevithick, the engineer (Camborne); William Barnes, poet and antiquarian (Dorchester); Edward Wilson, the explorer (Cheltenham); Robert Raikes, founder of Sunday Schools (Gloucester); Isaac Watts, Anglican hymn-writer (Southampton); Charles Gordon, soldier (Chatham); William Harvey, the physician who discovered the circulation of the blood (Folkestone); Thomas Paine, the philosopher (Thetford); and Thomas Gainsborough, portrait painter (Sudbury, Suffolk).

This particular aspect of environmental study – people – can be further developed by teachers making themselves aware of the writings of local authors. Is it possible, for instance, to teach in Dorchester (Dorset) and not bring Thomas Hardy to the children's notice, or in London and not use Pepys and Evelyn?

Within the classroom the teacher should attempt to support local excursions with small collections which are relevant to studies already under way or which are about to begin. These collections should seek to provoke enquiry and research. For example, a collection of old transport documents (i.e. photographs of trams, bus tickets, a timetable, a route map, and an Edwardian poster) might be displayed to encourage questions or as a means of consolidating knowledge already acquired.

Finally, let us assume that we are about to embark on a detailed study of the locality. We have everything in readiness. We have mounted a display or two, the children are eager and the headteacher willing. Is there anything else to think of? I would suggest that there is – two small points are often overlooked and yet which can, by their very omission, cause the whole programme to come to an abrupt halt. It is important, if children are to be expected to work out of doors, that they are given adequate materials to work with – and that includes a supply of pencils and something with which to sharpen them. It is always advisable, too, to make sure that the place to be visited is both open and able to receive the party. There is nothing worse than to arrive at a church to find that a funeral is in progress, or a museum to find the section needed is closed for redecoration!

3 Using the experience

Like all aspects of the school curriculum, an effective programme of local studies depends to a great extent upon the personal commitment of the teacher. We have seen in Chapter 2, the central part which the teacher plays in preparing for school visits and in having a clear (though flexible) view of the possibilities it offers to the class. Once the range of approaches has been identified, work with the children falls into three distinct stages.

Just as teachers need to prepare, so do children. It is essential that children know why they are visiting a particular site, how the visit links with work already under way (or about to begin), and the range of things which they will see and perhaps study. Of course, the approach adopted will be tempered to meet the age, aptitude, abilities, and interests of the children taking part. With groups of younger children, the preparation may simply take the form of a story involving people or an event associated with the site. Older children might study maps and photographs or be invited to prepare to undertake a specific topic on one aspect of the place they are to visit. For example, on visiting a castle children individually could make notes and sketches on such aspects as: window shapes (inside and out) and doorways; methods of defence; stairways and passageways; fireplaces; and facilities for preparing food. Visiting a large Victorian mansion would allow specific comparison to be made with our own times. Children could be invited to comment on such topics as: differences in the life of the people who lived 'above' and 'below' stairs, and reflect that if such distinctions exist today, how they are revealed; the effect of labour-saving devices on life-style; and the

Things of interest, my drawings and notes

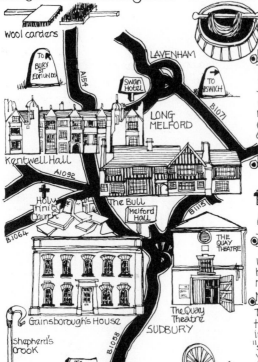

Wool carders

Dyeing the wool

LAVENHAM

SWAN HOTEL

LONG MELFORD

Kentwell Hall

Holy Trinity Church

The Bull

Melford Hall

THE QUAY THEATRE

Gainsborough's House

SUDBURY

The Quay Theatre

Shepherd's crook

19th C sheep shears

Shuttle for wool

one sheep in 5 mins.

Kentwell Hall
The Compton family started building the Hall in 1383 and they built the Holy Trinity Church in the 1400s. For nearly 200 years the Lady Chapel was used as a school and it still has multiplication tables painted on one wall.

Holy Trinity Church

The Bull
This is a 16th century inn which is supposed to be haunted. Someone was murdered there in 1648.

Melford Hall
This Hall was built in Tudor times and Elizabeth I visited it in 1578. It was said that "she was welcomed by 200 young gentlemen in white velvet, 300 in black and 1500 serving men." Beatrix Potter also stayed here a lot.

The Quay Theatre
This is in Sudbury. It was once an industrial building belonging to the River Stour Navigation Company. It was built in 1791 with red brick walls 2 feet thick.

Gainsborough's House
This is also in Sudbury and the painter Gainsborough was born here in 1727. He painted portraits of some of the wool merchants who lived in the area. The House is now open to the public.

The wool trade was the main industry in this part of East Anglia for nearly 700 years. The wool trade declined in the 18th century and farming took over but the areas around Long Melford and Sudbury have not changed all that much in the last 200 years. Places nearby are Cavendish, Clare and Lavenham. Castle Hedingham which is 7 miles from Sudbury was built in 1140 by Aubrey de Vere. The de Vere family came to England with William I in 1066

Figure 1 A road map on which places visited are recorded in words and pictures

changes that there have been in fashion, occupations, and leisure (with artefacts, portraits, and photographs being drawn upon for evidence). Additionally, have some of these objects remained unchanged since Victorian times? Why might this be? Which of the things that we take for granted would most surprise the inhabitants of a Victorian home?

It is at this preparation stage, then, that children need to be helped to decide how the information they are to collect is to be presented. Will each child be expected to produce a notebook, a drawing, an illustrated folder, a poster design, wall chart, or contribute to a slide sound presentation? Is it hoped to use the experience to provide opportunity for both descriptive and creative writing or as the theme for the next time that the class leads the school assembly? How much information will the children be given on site? If arrangements have been made for the children to meet the curator or attend a class on site, how is this likely to influence and shape their response?*

Whenever I take children (or adults) on a visit, I try to spend some time looking at the site, analysing it at a level appropriate to their age and experience. By regularly encouraging children to look at a site in a particular way, and by offering them a framework of questions, they will gradually become equipped to respond to buildings in the landscape. The simple survey sheets which I have included in this book can be developed by teachers for the children with whom they work and, suitably adapted, employed on almost any visit. They can be used to supplement specific areas of enquiry and to fill those uneasy moments which occur when waiting for a guide to arrive or for the coach to return.

Children will need to be shown 'how to look'. This is best accomplished through formal lessons within the classroom and information discussions while on visits. The questions which are central to such an approach may be listed, as follows.

1. *Why is the building here, and what is its function*? These two questions obviously relate to the children's perceptions of a building's current use. Even young children can 'read' shapes, enabling them to differentiate garage, castle, supermarket, castle and post office. The question 'Why is the building here?' may lead to some discussion about position and this may, in turn, raise geographic, social, or environmental issues. Why *are* castles so often built on a hill or in the loop of a river? Why are there no large departmental stores in a tiny village? Why are hypermarkets built out of town? Why in new towns

---

* This prompts the question: has the curator been briefed? And has he/she been told of the areas which are central to the study *these particular children* are undertaking?

TIME CHART Costumes

Knight in chain mail carrying a banner. about 1200. He might also have a shield.

Man wearing a hood. He would also have worn soft boots. 1280-1300

Man with small brimmed hat and embroidered tunic. Approximately 1400

Rich lady dressed in gown with a slashed skirt. It might have been decorated with gold and jewels. 1540

1670 Man with curly wig and a large hat

Gentleman in long top coat and long waistcoat with cravat. 1750

Young woman in simple high waisted dress. 1815

Man and a woman in about 1850. She is wearing a small straw hat with flowers. Her frock is made of patterned material. The man is wearing a top hat.

Man in around 1900. He is wearing a frock coat and a double breasted waistcoat with striped trousers. He has a walking stick which he is carrying.

A schoolgirl in the 1920s. She has a long waisted dress with a pleated skirt, a school hat and blazer and is carrying a school satchel.

This is me!

Figures 2 and 3 Children need to be able to set their findings within a historical time-scale. A time chart need not be a horizontal line – it can be represented much more dramatically

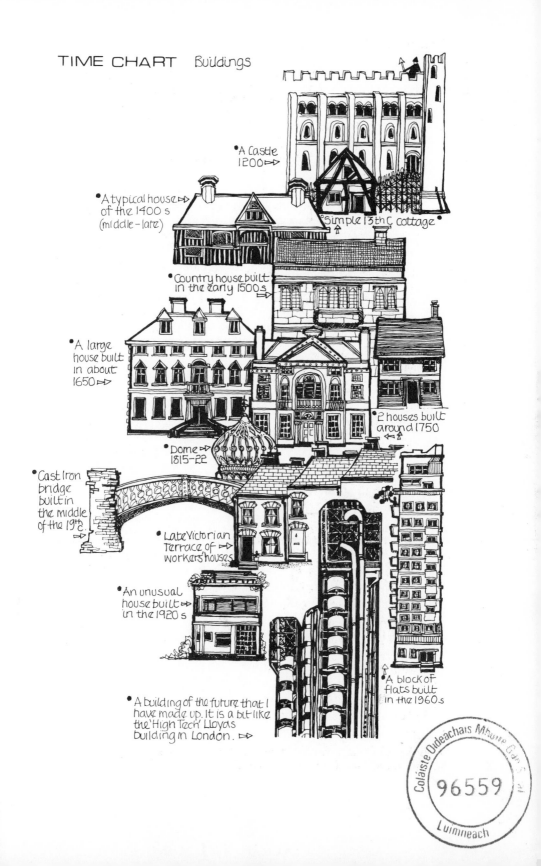

TIME CHART   Buildings

• A Castle 1200 ⇒

• A typical house of the 1400 s (middle – late)

• Simple 13th C cottage •

• Country house built in the early 1500 s ⇒

• A large house built in about 1650 ⇒

• 2 houses built around 1750 ⇐

• Dome ⇒ 1815 – 22

• Cast Iron bridge built in the middle of the 19th c. ⇒

• Late Victorian Terrace of workers' houses ⇒

• An unusual house built in the 1920 s

• A block of flats built in the 1960s

• A building of the future that I have made up. It is a bit like the 'High Tech' Lloyds building in London. ⇒

Chart 1

Materials for building
1. Walling

Stone	Try to discover if the stone was quarried locally – and if the quarry is still in use. If the stone was brought from a distant quarry, how was it transported? Use a map to show the extent of limestone in England (from Portland Bill in Dorset to the Cleveland Hills in Yorkshire).
Flint	Flint is found wherever there is chalk and is used in areas where stone is scarce. Flint can be 'knapped' (broken to give a smooth surface). Flint is often used with stone and brick to give evenness around windows and doors.
Puddingstone and septacia	A stone naturally formed from pebbles, flint, and sandstone. It varies in hardness.
Cobbles	Common in Norfolk, Suffolk, and Cumberland.
Granite	Occurs in Cornwall and parts of Scotland.
Marble	Often used to 'face' buildings to make them look more ornate.
Chalk	Common in Bedfordshire, Cambridgeshire, Devon, Dorset, Hampshire, Herefordshire, Lincolnshire, Norfolk, and Wiltshire.
Unbaked earth	Cob – a mixture of wet earth, lime, straw, gravel, or slate scraps, mixed with cow dung. It was often used as a 'daub' with wattles (woven sticks).
Earth	E.g. Hill forts, dykes.
Wood	How is the wood used? For a frame which is then unfilled with cob, or to 'face' completed walls?

is there a defined industrial area? Why were many early mills and factories built near waterways? Children who have been encouraged to look at the environment in which they live will begin to realize that buildings reflect the needs of living people. Once the need for the buildings has gone, buildings – and perhaps whole areas – tend to decay. Sometimes a change of need will result in a building being used to fulfil a different function – a church becomes a museum, a weaver's cottage an elegant home, and a monastic grain barn a place to keep farm vehicles.

2. *How old is the building? Who built it? Has it been extended? If so, when?* These questions stem from question 1. Young children have a very undeveloped concept of time. Dates, of themselves, mean little. Nevertheless, it is important to try to help children develop a sense of historical sequence. One way of doing this is consciously to relate all historical topics to a time-line. This could be on display in the classroom; children could also make their own. As information is acquired about places visited, it could be translated (in picture form) to the individual class and charts.

Brick	Common in Roman times, but its widespread use in England dates from about 1200 when it was introduced to England from the Low Countries.
'Rendered walling'	A term used to describe a building whose walls have been coated with cob or plaster and, more recently, pebble-dash.

2. *Roofing*

Thatch	Reed is commonly used in East Anglia, Huntingdon, and the Isle of Ely; straw (from wheat, barley, oats, rye) is used across much of the rest of Britain.
Stone	Split into slates, particularly common in areas where limestone is easily obtainable.
Slate	Much of the slate used in Britain was quarried in Wales; some was also obtained from the Lake District.
Tiles	Old tiles were made of clay. Most modern tiles are made from coloured concrete.

3. *Other materials*

Iron	For gates, hinges, gutterings and drains, decorations, and girders.
Glass	The manufacture of plate-glass dates from 1773. Until this date sheets of glass were small and expensive to produce.
Modern materials	E.g. concrete, plastic, and sheet-glass.

3. *What materials have been used?* Space prevents the inclusion of a detailed analysis of building materials.* The chart indicates something of the range which could be covered.

4. *Specific questions* Questions about materials can be supplemented with questions of a more specific nature. The list which follows is not meant to be exhaustive, but serve to indicate the types of question which prompt enquiry: what is the shape of the roof? Has the building been decorated in any way? Is there a chimney-stack? Where is it positioned? What is the shape of the windows? And the doors? Specific questions such as these should be used to encourage children to refer to books and charts and to use library resources intelligently.

5. *What can be learned from the inside of the building?* Additional questions which could be included here are: How is it now used? Is it used for the purpose for which it was built? Are there any strange stories which relate to it?

* The Bibliography in Appendix 2 includes a section on vernacular architecture.

Children's personal 'discoveries' (a term I prefer to the word 'answer', which implies a neat correctness rarely found in any building) can be recorded in words, sketches, or photographs. They can be supported by maps and plans and any other information which they find intriguing.

In approaching a study in this way, vocabulary will inevitably be extended. To classify or describe a particular building will require mastery of specific and technical language. In the chapters which follow I have indicated some of the words and phrases which children might need to master. This approach, which is founded upon the belief that children can be shown how to look and how to respond to looking, will not come from one short lesson in school. It is a continuous activity which should extend throughout a child's school life.

Preparation within the classroom serves to alert children to the types of activity that they might undertake on site. Visits are most likely to be successful when children are able to respond at a personal (rather than group) level. This will not mean that the range of response will be impossibly wide. Suitably encouraged, the great majority of children will want to make their own notes and sketches. Sharp pencils, a supply of paper, and a sketchboard will therefore be required by each child.

Accurate observation and recording can also be fostered by providing children with crayons (or oil pastels) and large sheets of sugar paper (A3, A2). Working in crayon prevents over-concentration upon fussy details. By offering a choice from a range of coloured papers children can also be shown how to choose a tone which enhances the chosen subject – steely grey for sketches of knights, brown for castle ruins, blues and greens for seascapes, red for Tudor brickwork, etc.

Crayons are also invaluable because they can be used for textured rubbings. For this, detail paper will be required. The surface from which a rubbing is to be taken must be first dusted with a soft cloth. The detail paper is placed over the brass, stone, or plaque and held in place either with strips of Sellotape or lead weights – though on some vertical surfaces additional hands are the best method; the paper should be taut and pucker-free. The crayon is rubbed in firm, even strokes over the paper covering the actual design, all the strokes being made in the same direction. When the rubbing has been completed, the paper is carefully removed. This technique may be used to obtain texture rubbings of tombstones, brasses, wall plaques, commemorative plates, and decorative brickwork and ironwork – in fact anything which has texture.

Rubbings may also be taken on detail paper with white crayon. To make the design reappear is quite simple: on return to school, pin the rubbing on to a flat surface and brush cold-water dyes, Ebony Stain, or black fountain-pen ink (not indian ink) over the whole paper. The white waxed areas will resist the wet colour, making the design appear against a black surround. When the stain has dried, cut round the rubbing and paste on to a mounting-board.

It is necessary to obtain permission before rubbings are taken of church brasses. Indiscriminate rubbing can do irreparable damage.

Used sensitively, tape recorders and cameras can provide a valuable additional dimension to a visit; however, recording a guide or the comments of a local resident should not be seen as a replacement for notebook and pencil. Replayed in school, recordings should be used to enhance and extend the children's written response. Pictures (slides or prints) provide a similar opportunity. In this connection, children should be made responsible both for photography and recording. Pocket mini-recorders and 35 mm autofocus cameras are comparatively inexpensive to buy and to service. In quantity, both should be part of the basic equipment of every school – primary and secondary.

All that I have written so far consciously avoids the most difficult aspect of environmental studies. To what extent should we direct the children's eyes to this or that exhibit in a museum, or this or that feature of a castle? To say 'Look at this and draw it' is as narrowing as the Dotheboys Hall approach of 'Winders, clean 'em'! Do children need to record the same thing in the same way, so that we can say, 'This they have learned'? In every group there seems to be some children who appear to depend upon a given list of exhibits to make notes on – this smacks of despair. Might it not be that we need to discover for these children another way of looking, giving them another vehicle (or technique) through which to express themselves?

It has also been suggested that the value of any school visit, any happening, lies in the impact which it has upon each child, and this cannot necessarily be measured, marked, painted, drawn, or written about. For me, this view is rather too romantic (particularly at a time, perhaps, when education tends to be evaluated in ways more in keeping with the market-place than the schoolroom). Nevertheless, I can wonder at the skill of a Norman stonemason, gaze with awe at a Leonardo cartoon, or be transported by a Mozart symphony – but please don't ask me to draw my experiences!

However well the children have been prepared, the teacher's role on visits should never be that of a passive watcher and minder. The best model that children can be given is that of an enquiring and inquisitive adult. Teachers should look for things which might be useful for follow-up work in school; these will include postal guides

(Yellow Pages, Thomson directories), plans, maps, photographs, posters, and guidebooks. Equally important are things 'found' – corks from fishermen's nets, an interesting stone, some pottery shards, the basket-maker's reeds, a fossil, a nail from the smith, a withy from a fence-maker.

On return to school, the visit should be discussed in detail before any follow-up work is attempted. Children have a tremendous need to verbalize – yet too often the first thing they have to do is 'write it up'.

The discussion could begin by encouraging each child to talk about the things they saw, smelt, touched, heard, and where appropriate tasted. This may lead to an awareness on the children's part of what they wanted to communicate about the experience. Is it best to use words, to make a model, or paint a picture? For each of the children there will be a different way, uniquely their own, and a way which allows for emotion to show through their work. This means of course that the classroom should contain a wide range of materials, so that children are not frustrated by being unable to find the very things they need to communicate how they really feel.

For some children the experience of a visit will be described in words, their descriptions attempting to capture something of the atmosphere in a past age. After visiting Oxburgh Hall, in Norfolk, Ralph, aged 9, wrote:

I watched the wood fire crackle and flicker and the candle melt away. The wind was howling and beating at the shutters. I walked to the fire place where the flames lept up the big chimney. I poured some ale and drank it, listening to my Father talking about Cromwell. 'Up to bed now', said my Mother. I climbed the big staircase to my room. I peered out of the window. The soldier was still on guard.

Alice, aged 8, also used an imaginative approach; following on a visit to a castle whose owners re-create the past for children by appearing in medieval costume, she wrote:

Upon the scene there came to greet us fair Lady Joan, all garbed black velvet and silk. She said her Knight would come to show us deeds of strength and courage. Upon that, she led us, jewels sparkling, to the loo.

The writing continued, in similar quaintly turned phrases, for fifteen paragraphs.

Not all children enjoy writing in this imaginative way; some prefer a more factual approach. Jane, aged 7, visited Dedham, in Essex, to see Willy Lot's Cottage. She was particularly impressed with the weather:

Clouds, dull black trying to spread themselves across the sky. White grey ones, running away from the black. A storm is coming. It's evening. The clouds are dark and dull.

Anna, aged 8, uses her account to describe in detail how a house she visited was constructed:

We saw a very old cruck house. A cruck house is made with oak beams like this. Two beams are put upwards making an arch. Then a long pole is put on the top and two other poles are put on each side. There can be as many arches as you like. On top of the three poles there are rafters, on top of the rafters, thatch. One end of the cruck house is for the people, the other end is for the animals. The cruck house I saw had a salt box in the fireplace. Salt was precious so the King put a tax on it and to keep the salt dry people would put a salt box near the fire. The person sitting nearest the salt is the most important person. The cruck house had a witch post to keep evil spirits away.

James, aged 9, is even more concerned with facts:

We went to the lighthouse. The keeper talked about the engine. Then we went upstairs and saw where the emergency light was housed. We went up some much steeper steps to the big light. It was made up of little prisms. There was a spare light on the side so if the other went off the spare one came on. The light flashed three times every twenty seconds. The light was of 10,000 candle power. The light would cost £30,000 to replace.

Such carefully structured presentation does not come easily. It takes time to develop. It therefore follows that the somewhat inconsequential approach which characterizes the work of the younger child must be encouraged and respected. Manny, aged 7, visited Hampton Court Palace; he wrote:

It was built in 1514 for Thomas Wolsey and King Henry the VIII got jealous and angry so he gave it to him to make him happy. When Thomas Wolsey had it he had 500 servants. But Henry was not happy.
Then we went back to school. We got the number 4 bus to get to school and we got the train to get the bus.

Other children will enjoy presenting their ideas in a form of irregular verse. Peter, aged 8, wrote:

I am a little mill mouse,
And I live in Draper's Mill.
When the miller's milling,
I watch the wheels turn round,
I watch the grain go in one end,
And come out the other, ground.

Writing of this quality and range does not occur accidentally. Although the actual journey will feature in the writing (as it does in an example included here), the teacher's task is to concentrate the children's minds and direct their purpose towards recapturing in words and pictures the 'flavour' of the place that has been visited.

Children will also need to be helped to understand that the style of writing which they adopt will be shaped by the way in which it is to be used. The style appropriate to a personal guidebook or diary will be somewhat different from that of a piece of descriptive verse about a canal, written to be read against the background of tinkling percussion in the morning assembly; the tight economy of words required on a poster; or the accuracy of language needed to explain a graph.

The response to any visit, be it reflected through words, music, painting, graphing, model-making, printing, drama, or music, will be at several levels. Every child responds as an individual, as a member of a group, and of a class. The completed work should reflect this

Display provides a valuable commentary on children's discoveries. This work, by 5–8-year-olds, followed upon visits to museums and practical school-based experiments around the theme of 'air'

Hampton Court. A display by 9-year-olds. A visit may result in the production of unexpected drawings. These 5- and 6-year-olds met a horse which had belonged to Lord Mountbatten. Their pictures are shown here

range of response. For example, every child could keep a diary, a notebook, or compile study sheets to record their personal response. Experiences shared and work corporately completed can be carefully mounted in group study books. In addition, much can be achieved through classroom display.

Display, should aim at communicating something of the total experience: 'We went to Edinburgh . . . This is what we saw . . . This is what we learned.' Every display should project through the quality of the material presented something of the excitement of learning.

We can enhance the appearance of the children's work by careful selection of their pictures, models, and poetry and prose. I don't think it necessary to mount every piece of work, though it is important that whenever possible something from each child is included. The selection need not be the teacher's – children can be just as ruthless in their rejection of material. The following simple hints, however, may prove useful to whoever makes the final choice.

(a) Cover the display board with backing paper or fabric which will blend with the topic being featured, e.g. deep or olive green will give an attractive backing for rubbings worked in gold crayon, blue for seascapes, and brown for architectural pen-and-ink studies. All types of paper are suitable for covering display boards, though pastel paper is perhaps the most effective.

(b) Trim and mount the pictures before display.

(c) Marry children's work with material from other sources, e.g. an artist's impression of a village displayed near a child's drawing. This means, then, that photographs, post-cards, and newspaper cuttings should be seen as valuable additions to the children's recorded experiences.

(d) Use a staple tacker or pin pusher to mount the work – four large brass drawing-pins in the corners of a small pen-and-ink sketch hardly help it be seen as a thing of beauty.

(e) Display notices should be uniform throughout (and preferably similar for all displays in one classroom at any one time). Felt pens are so much easier to handle than the more traditional lettering media, although they do not give the delicate flow of line obtainable with a lettering pen.

(f) Include books in the display. These may be books make by the children or reference books which have been used in the study.

It has been said that the aim of the primary school teacher should be to make 'the classroom a child's place, a workshop, a place which is his own'. How better can we achieve this ideal than by using the children's experiences for creative work of all kinds, which within the classroom environment are extended and deepened?

4 Where we live

The area in which the school is situated, be this in a rural hamlet or busy city, provides the ideal starting-point for environmental studies. However 'new' the town, however decayed and uninspiring the surroundings, the school and the houses and flats in which the children live provide an appropriate starting-point to understanding. *This* street, *this* particular house or block of flats, *this* corner-shop, *this* market-place, *this* bus shelter, and *this* school, form the backdrop to which each child relates and is the environment in which he or she moves. It is comfortably familiar; it is accepted – often to the extent that it is taken for granted and ignored.

However environmental studies are to be used (as entry into history and geography or as a subject worthy of study in its own right), the local area should not be spurned. Nor should it be studied for a short period and then neglected. It is a theme which merits a place in the curriculum of each primary school year.

The problem of devoting a chapter to 'Where we live' is that a study of the immediate locality embraces many of the topics which are covered elsewhere in this book. For example, it is impossible to study an area without touching upon the principal buildings within it (like the church, village, town or city hall, railway or bus station, school, hospital, village shop or supermarket). I will therefore attempt to do little more than indicate entry points which can be supplemented with ideas drawn from other chapters.

I am also conscious that there is a very real difference between living in a village and living in a town. A village is usually clearly defined with a character of its own. In comparison, towns are

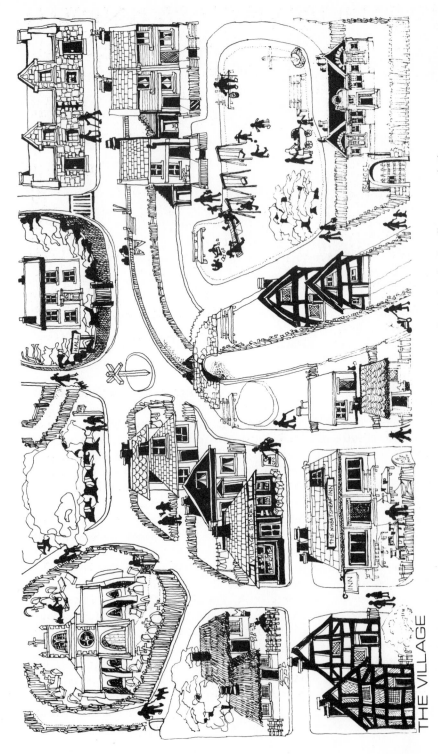

THE VILLAGE

A group map of the local area – each member of the group contributing to the final collage or painting

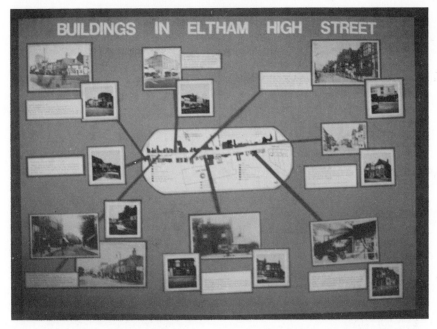

Recording the locality. A display by a group of students (18-year-olds) in the first weeks of teacher training

anonymous places, one community blending imperceptibly with the next.

These reservations made, let me suggest how the streets around the school can provide the starting-point for study. For this, a map is essential. This 'starter' map, which need be little more than a large-scale drawing taken from a local street atlas, can be used to provide material for an illustrated wall map to which all the children can contribute. With older children, the picture map could be used as an introduction to conventional map-making (using Ordnance Survey symbols) and to a study of the area through maps and plans obtained from the county or borough archivist.

Photographs, postcards, and historic prints collected while the study is under way and mounted on to the pictorial wall map can be supplemented with children's notes and drawings. This might result in children identifying themselves with particular parts of the map: 'This is Mike's house', 'This is Akbar's uncle's café', and 'This is the farm where we go to see the cows'.

As children explore their immediate environment an attempt could be made to 'date' the buildings. This might be through a wall plaque, the manufacturer's stamp on an iron girder, or a document or a map or print in the local library. Churches and chapels were often built at the same time as the large Victorian estates they serve, and usually bear the date on which they were dedicated (and the estate developed).

As the streets in the immediate vicinity of school are studied a method of looking and recording can be developed. To do this successfully a simple framework of open-ended questions should be devised; for example:

1. What kind of buildings are there?
   Are they mainly industrial, agricultural, commercial, or residential? Do most of the buildings (in this street, square) have a similar function?
2. Are any of the buildings particularly interesting or important?
3. Would it be worth while to analyse one of the buildings in detail (see Chapter 3)?
4. What materials have been commonly used in the buildings?
5. Is there any evidence to suggest that there has been any change in use?

Question 5 merits detailed examination. Buildings, like human beings, have a life cycle of creation and decay. Sometimes decay (caused by weathering, age, or vandalism) is halted by repair, sometimes buildings have their life extended by being converted to a use for which they were not constructed. Again, some buildings do not decay, but are swept away by developers long before they have begun to age. This cycle is easily identified in most communities. The empty shop, the open-roofed barn, the glossy supermarket, the advertisement hoardings around a weed-covered waste, the temporary car-park, and the building-site all serve to indicate something of the change and continuity of human affairs. When inviting children to identify elements in this cycle, attention should also be drawn to the continual evolution of properties which is simultaneously taking place – a car-port alongside a somewhat seedy Edwardian villa, a garage next to a seventeenth-century cottage, windows indicating a roof conversion, secondary glazing, fuel tanks in each of the gardens of a Victorian terrace, or 'gentrified' council housing.

The slow evolution of a community can also be examined by noting its areas of dereliction. Stretches of wasteland in a town might have been caused because factories have closed, or because slum housing has been swept away or the land has been long used in a way which, in contemporary terms, is irrelevant (e.g. a cavalry training barracks in Colchester, an armaments centre in Woolwich, and docklands in East London, Chatham, or Liverpool). Derelict land may be contrasted with that which is described as 'neglected', e.g. an overgrown and uncared for cemetery, a railway line which has been closed but not cleared, a boarded factory awaiting refurbishment and a new tenant.

When studying 'waste' land, children could be encouraged to suggest a reason for its present condition or provoked to think about how it might best be developed for community use. The mapping of areas of dereliction could be accompanied by any ecological changes which have been noticed. What happens when a site is left to nature? What kinds of plants, birds, and insects return?

Land in decay can be plotted and graphed against land in use. How many dwellings are there in a defined area around school, how many shops, factories, garages, public houses, and banks? How much land is available for recreation and leisure? The types of classification are limitless: how many houses, flats, maisonettes, and bungalows? How many different types of retail outlet? How many of these offer goods? How many offer services?

A similar study could be made in a rural community. Here classification may centre on how the land is used for farming: is it used for grazing? What type of animals graze on it? Is it used for crops (rape, oats, fruit, vegetables), woodland, or left fallow?

Whereas the area selected for study in an urban environment will tend to be somewhat indiscriminately determined (e.g. by the rectangle formed by four mainroads), a village study can be based upon the parish boundaries. This will mean that the shape of the village can be analysed. For example, has it grown up around a hill top or does it nestle in a valley bottom? Is it a village in which the older houses are grouped around a village green or is it a 'linear' village, which has no centre and where the houses and shops straggle along the two side of a road? Is there evidence that the village was created to serve the needs of a powerful landowner (e.g. Chatsworth, Derbyshire), an industrial site (e.g. a mine, factory, or quarry), a religious foundation (e.g. Walsingham, Norfolk), a fortress (e.g. Corfe, Dorset), or at the cross-roads of a trade source (e.g. Banbury, Oxford)? Is there evidence that the village has declined in importance? Is it now smaller than it once was (e.g. the 'wool villages' of eastern England)? This, in turn, could lead to an investigation of villages in the immediate area which have 'disappeared' (over 2,000 villages have vanished since medieval times).

It would be possible to adapt this approach to many urban areas: 'We live in Kirkstall. When did our village become part of a larger town, and why?' Down the centuries economic and political considerations have turned many small hamlets into large towns and sprawling cities. Thus the following questions are also appropriate:

SURVEY SHEET

AREA VISITED   Barnard Castle, Durham

BUILDING/PLACE   Small Town

Date   End April 1988

<u>Things of interest, my drawings and notes.</u>

<u>Barnard Castle</u> is an old town that stands on the banks of the River Tyne. The town grew up around the Castle that was built here. The land was given to Guy de Baliol by William Rufus and the first castle was built before 1100. This castle was rebuilt in 1150 but it is now a ruin which covers nearly 6½ acres. Before the Normans there was no settlement but the <u>Roman Road</u> from Bowes to Bicester crossed the river here. Now there is an old stone bridge. (16th century I think). There is a market place with a <u>Market Cross</u> built in 1747 by Thomas Breaks who lived in the town. Nearby is <u>Blagroves House</u> a 16th century inn. Some think Oliver Cromwell stopped here in 1648 on his way to Richmond. Close by is the <u>King's Head</u> where Charles Dickens stayed in 1838. The grandest building is the <u>Bowes Museum</u> built by John Bowes and his wife Josephine. It is built of local stone and looks a bit like a French Chateau. It houses collections of paintings, lace, costume, furniture dolls and many other things. In the <u>Norman Church</u> at Barnard Castle is a memorial to 143 locals who died of cholera in two months in 1849 and to a man who died at Balaclava.

Blagroves House

Column

Plan

Market Cross

Bowes Museum

Figure 5 Survey of a town – Barnard Castle

1. Did the settlement expand as a result of new methods of communication? (Crewe – railways)
2. Did it grow up when it became a regional government centre? (Ludlow was the seat of the Council of the Marches of Wales; and York of the Council of the North)
3. Did the settlement grow around a river-crossing? (Bristol)

If the settlement is a port, did it develop because of a specific trade (e.g. Manchester – cotton; Southampton – wool; Bristol – slaves) or because of some other factor (e.g. Chatham and Plymouth – naval dockyards)? Did the settlement develop around a spa (e.g. Bath, Brighton, Tonbridge Wells)?

Of course, some of our towns may be traced to pre-Roman or Celtic settlements and, in this event, we are rather left struggling in the mists of antiquity. Place names, however, provide useful clues. Royal charters are another valuable pointer to urban development and serve to indicate how the status of a community has changed over the years. For example, Northleach, in Gloucestershire, was granted a charter in 1227, some eighty years before Newcastle upon Tyne; but today few people would be able to pinpoint Northleach on a map, whereas Newcastle has an international reputation.

All of the evidence collected as a result of enquiries of the type suggested above will indicate when the first people began to live in the area and how slowly (or quickly) the settlement developed. Population statistics (the first accurate figures date from 1801) and local maps will also help define the probable limits during any given period.

The streets themselves might well provide evidence of historical development such as the direction they run in, even their names. For example, Fleet Street, in London, reminds us of the river which was for years 'the city sewer', while Brook Street in many small towns and villages follows the curves of long dried up springs.

An alphabetical collection of local street names may provide much material for research, particularly if the town or village has existed for several centuries. The names might relate to commerce, to industry, the geographical limits of the settlement, its famous citizens, or its church or baronial property. For example: Beau Street, Westgate Street (Bath); Palace Street, Castle Street, Military Road (Canterbury); Botchergate (Carlisle); Northgate, Watergate, Foregate, White Friars (Chester); Milk Street (Exeter); Beauchamp Hill (Leamington); Horsefair Street, Haymarket, Highcross (Leicester); Sheep Street, Mercers Row (Northampton); Castle Meadow, Tombland, Maddermarket (Norwich); Woolpack Lane (Nottingham); St Aldates, Cornmarket (Oxford); Mayflower Street, Sidney Street (Plymouth);

Chart 2

A note on place names

Beck	Road (Norwegian)
Borough, Burgh, Bury	Fortified camp, house, or town
Bourne	A small river (e.g. Winterbourne, the place where a river runs only in winter)
Breck	Hill
Bridge	A crossing-place
By	Village
Caster, Cester, Chester	A fortified place
Combe	Valley
Cot, Cott, Cotte	Cottage or place of shelter
Dale	Valley
Den	A valley or a place where animals are grazed
Don	A hill
Fell	A hill
Field	Open place (e.g. Sheffield, a place for pasturing sheep)
Ford	A crossing-place
Gill	A valley
Ham	A meadow, home-place, or a village
Hay	An enclosure in a forest clearing
Head	Implies (sometimes) ancient religious link (e.g. Gateshead, ritual associated with goat)
Ing, Ingham	'The followers of' (e.g. Reading, the place of the followers of Reada; Walsingham, home of the followers of Waels)

Holywell Hill, Verulam Road (St Albans); Abbey Foregate, Murivance Town Walls (Shrewsbury); and Cutler Street, Poultry, Jewry Street, Pepys Street, Stone Cutters Street, Sea Coal Lane (City of London).

Some thought will also need to be given to how buildings may best be studied. Obviously they provide much material for drawing and model-making. But it would be short-sighted to suggest that the whole group follows the same approach. By encouraging children to concentrate upon specific areas of study, both the individual and the group benefit. We could, for example, take children to draw a Nash terrace or a village high street, and return to school with thirty almost identical sketches. How much richer the work can be if some of the children concentrate on doorways, while others work on windows, carved motifs, or decorated ironwork.

If this is applied to a wider-based survey, individual studies could be made by some children of such features as chimney-pots, doors, windows, shop fronts, street lights, commemorative plaques, statues, post-boxes, old advertisements (some buildings in industrial backstreets still proclaim the wonders of long forgotten tonics and

Lake	Water, usually fed by a stream
Lan, Llan	A place associated with a saint (used as a prefix)
Lay, Leigh, Ley	An open space
Port	A market-place
Scale	A hut
Slack	A valley
Spital	A hospital, a place for lepers
Stock, Stoke	A place
Stow	A holy place (e.g. Felixstowe, the holy place of St Felix)
Street	A paved way, road. This may be used as a prefix (streat, strat) (e.g. Streeton, Stratford)
Tarn	Small lake
Thorpe	Hamlet
Thwaite	Clearing
Toft	Homestead
Ton, Tun	Farm or manor
Tre	A farm (usually a prefix)
Well	Place with a spring
Wick (coastal)	A bay
Wick (inland)	Buildings, often a farm with cows
Worthy	An enclosure round a house

In addition to this basic list, children might look for evidence of Norman-French on a local map (e.g. Beaumaris, Rievaulx, Dieulacres) or places with religious (e.g. Abbotsbury), royal (e.g. Bere Regis), or military associations (e.g. Temple Combe – the Knights Templars).

elixirs). Others might make detailed notes on changing architectural styles.

Studies of this kind will inevitably require that early maps are compared with their modern counterparts. Such comparisons will indicate something of the changing patterns of settlement and land utilization; the development of roads and railways; the decay and expansion of communities; and the growth of estates and their division or disappearance. Copies of early local maps (e.g. maps by Speed, Pont, and their successors) are obtainable through the local archivist, county reference library, or museum service. The Ordnance Survey maps of Prehistoric, Iron Age, Roman, Dark Age, Monastic and Medieval Britain will also prove useful.

Local studies whether in town or country will uncover elements which indicate the relationship over time between people and their environment. The elements will be revealed in many forms. The relationship may be reflected through the existence or ruins of buildings (religious, military, domestic, industrial); through almshouses and school foundations; through town crests and village

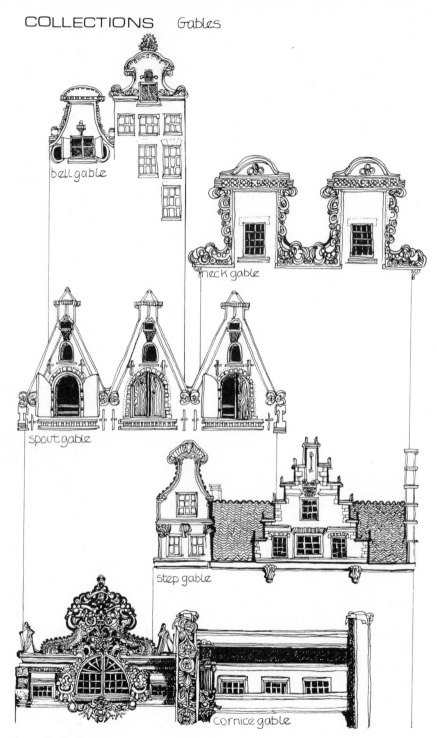

bell gable

neck gable

spout gable

step gable

cornice gable

Figure 6 Collections – house detail

signs; through the principal occupations and crafts of the area; and even through the signboards of public houses which may vividly throw light on English social history.

Thus we can study a community through the people who live in it. Although families have become more mobile since the Second World War, grandparents still enjoy a prominent place in the lives of young children. If the family has lived in the area for many years, grandparents can contribute much of value to the study, portable tape recorders being used to record impressions of life fifty or sixty years ago. If supporting photographs can be borrowed, they may be used as source materials for children's pictures (dress, transport, and housing) or carefully mounted to support their own written work.

Oral sources should never be despised, particularly as older people often remember their own childhood quite clearly. Of course, if they remember stories told them about the neighbourhood by their grandparents, we may have managed to span 130 years or more.*

Oral history can be extended through the use of selected extracts from local diarists and biographers. Use of such sources can help deepen children's understanding of the area in which they live, particularly if the extracts chosen comment upon buildings, statues, and customs particular to their town or village (see Chapter 7).

Local people can also give the children some understanding of services which they perform for the community - e.g. in such fields as electricity, gas and water supply, law and order, and communications. On the whole, public services are prepared to co-operate very closely with schools. For example, I have taken 5- and 6-year-olds to a police stables, 7-year-olds to a fire station, 8-year-olds to a river police HQ, 9-year-olds to the Post Office Tower, and 10-year-olds to an electricity generating station. In each case the numbers were kept as small as possible, several visits being made so that as many children as possible could benefit from the experience.

Of course, not all workplaces are suitable for parties of young children to visit. Usually LEAs as well as public service departments follow a code of regulations, designed to protect teacher and taught. However, most public services are able to provide some facilities for school parties usually in the form of visual aids, film strips, loops, charts, and booklets. Often speakers will be prepared to come to school to talk about their work, and while this perhaps lacks the

---

* In 1969 I happened to meet Sir Harry Verney in the chapel at Claydon House, in Buckinghamshire. He was nearing his hundredth birthday. He spoke at length to me, telling me of his boyhood, of Florence Nightingale and the stories she told of the Crimean War; Florence had spent much time in the house. An outstanding example of oral history.

COLLECTIONS Inn Signs

Religious

Country

Royal

Animal

Travel

History

Local Interest

Figure 7 Collections – Inn signs

Chart 3

A note on inn signs

The signs for inns, hotels, and public houses take three forms – a flat painted board, a model, and occasionally a 'gallows' which spans the road; inn signs could be classified under the following headings:

1. *Royal*	e.g. The Crown, The King's Head, The Royal Oak, The Rose, Royal Standard, Black Prince
2. *Baronial*	e.g. The Red Lion (John of Gaunt), The Bear and Ragged Staff (Warwick), Eagle and Child (Earl of Derby), Green Dragon (Pembroke)
3. *People*	e.g. John Kennedy, Sir Winston Churchill, Marquess of Granby, Sir Christopher Wren, Captain Cook, Charlie Chaplin, Amy Johnson
4. *Events*	e.g. Trafalgar, Waterloo, Mafeking, Everest
5. *Myths and legends*	e.g. The Mermaid, The Dragon, The Phoenix, George and the Dragon, Unicorn
6. *Oddities*	e.g. The World Turned Upside Down, The Honest Lawyer, The Finny Cook
7. *Living creatures*	e.g. The White Horse, The Elephant, The Lion, The Cat, The Bee, The Eagle, The Ostrich
8. *Sports*	e.g. Fighting Cocks, Bird in the Hand (hawking), Dog and Duck (shooting), The Cricketers, The Two Wrestlers, The Starting-Gate (racing), The Jolly Fisherman, The Chequered Flag (motor sport)
9. *Travel Pilgrimage*	e.g. The Two Compasses (corruption of 'God Encompasses Us'), The Crossed Keys (St Peter), St Thomas of Canterbury, The Turk's Head (Crusades)
The Age of Wool	e.g. The Pack Horse, The Carter, The Woolpack, The Waggon and Horses (or Oxen)
Turnpikes	e.g. The Tollgate, Halfway House (i.e. between two stages), Journey's End.
Coaching	e.g. The Four-in-Hand, The Coach and Horses, The Horse and Groom
Steam	e.g. Great Eastern, The Railway Arms, The Rocket, Station Hotel
Air	e.g. The Propeller, The Merlin (aero-engine), The Flying Lancaster, Who'd Have Thought It? (space travel)
10. *Occupations*	e.g. The Pedlar, The Wheatsheaf (corn-chandlers), The Miller, Adam and Eve (booksellers), The Horseshoes (smiths, farmers), The Golden Fleece (wool merchants)

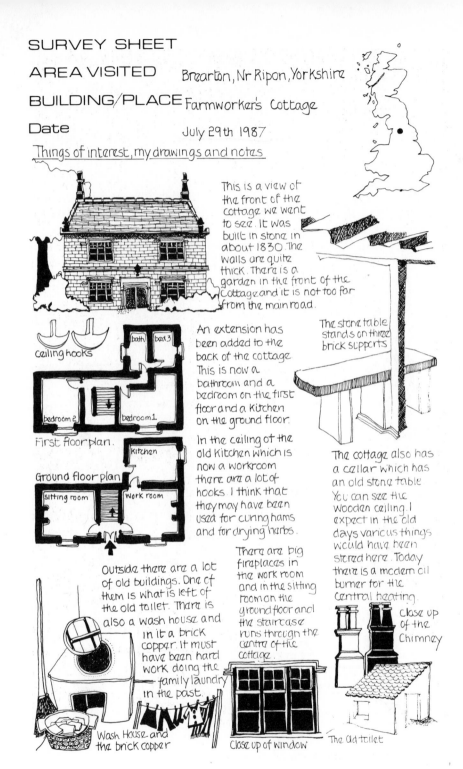

SURVEY SHEET

AREA VISITED   Brearton, Nr Ripon, Yorkshire

BUILDING/PLACE Farmworker's Cottage

Date   July 29th 1987

Things of interest, my drawings and notes

This is a view of the front of the cottage we went to see. It was built in stone in about 1830. The walls are quite thick. There is a garden in the front of the cottage and it is not too far from the main road.

ceiling hooks

First floor plan.

Ground floor plan

An extension has been added to the back of the cottage. This is now a bathroom and a bedroom on the first floor and a kitchen on the ground floor.

In the ceiling of the old kitchen which is now a workroom there are a lot of hooks. I think that they may have been used for curing hams and for drying herbs.

The stone table stands on three brick supports

The cottage also has a cellar which has an old stone table. You can see the wooden ceiling. I expect in the old days various things would have been stored here. Today there is a modern oil burner for the central heating.

Outside there are a lot of old buildings. One of them is what is left of the old toilet. There is also a wash house and in it a brick copper. It must have been hard work doing the family laundry in the past.

There are big fireplaces in the work room and in the sitting room on the ground floor and the staircase runs through the centre of the cottage.

Close up of the Chimney

Wash House and the brick copper

Close up of window

The Old toilet

Figure 8 Survey of a house – Brearton

Children learn by meeting people: 6-year-olds being introduced to the world of make-up and theatre

significance of a school visit to the workplace, it does provide a tangible link with the real world.

An appreciation of the individual character of town and village is gained only by close personal acquaintance. When a place has a distinctive 'flavour', it is useful to try to analyse its uniqueness, so that comparisons can be made. A group of children from Liverpool, for example, may find it worth while to compare their city with Dunwich (Suffolk) or Rye or Winchelsea (Sussex), once the most prosperous ports in England.

The urban scene has as much to offer to the teacher as a castle, a cathedral, or medieval manor house. History is all around us, whether our school overlooks the ruins of a Norman keep or an industrial wasteland. All we need to do is to learn how to use it.

5 Places of worship

In almost every age and across every continent human beings have established within their area of settlement special places where they may practise their religious beliefs. In Britain this is reflected in the remains of wooden and stone henges and Roman temples, Christian churches and chapels, synagogues, and the temples, mosques and religious meeting-places of more recent settlers. It follows therefore that buildings specifically designed for worship confirm and comment upon the hopes, beliefs, and ideals of the people who first built them, as well as those of subsequent generations, who have devoted themselves to their upkeep and maintenance.

Although Christianity came to Britain in Roman times, St Augustine's mission to Kent (597) is usually taken as marking the establishment of the church in England. In the centuries which followed church and state became inextricably intertwined.

Today the church exercises far less temporal power than it did during certain periods of the more distant past, but the influence it once enjoyed continues to be reflected through local customs and the ceremonies of state. Wells continue to be blessed, parish boundaries continue to be 'beaten', ploughs and farm equipment continue to be taken to church in order that the crops will be plentiful, and bishops continue to sit in the House of Lords – all of these practices may appear ephemeral, but they point to long-held beliefs and practices.

This suggests that however conscious we become of the multi-cultural nature of contemporary society, we are failing in our task if we ignore the contribution which an analysis of the church can make to local studies. In many communities churches will be the oldest and

SURVEY SHEET

AREA VISITED   Tissington, Derbyshire

BUILDING/PLACE   St Mary's Church

Date   21st September 1987

Things of interest, my drawings and notes

St Mary's Church is in the village of Tissington and it dates from about 1100. In the churchyard there are a lot of graves. There is a base of a Saxon cross and nearby is the tomb of the Allsop family (one died when the Titanic sank in 1912.)

rough plan of the church

The porch of the church has an early Norman doorway and above the door some geometric patterns and two human figures are roughly carved. Inside the church there are lots of monuments to the Fitzherbert family who restored the church in Victorian times although a lot of the original Norman building is still there. There are Norman arches and a circular Norman font. The font has some very strange carvings.

The Font

Arch

Figures from the Fitzherbert memorial tomb (1619)

Details of the carvings

Tissington is also famous for its "well dressing" ceremony which takes place on Ascension Day. It is a thanksgiving for the blessing of pure water. The well dressings are made of flower petals, leaves, twigs etc which are pressed into wet clay making coloured pictures of scenes from The Bible. The ceremony may date from the 14th century when Tissington escaped the Black Death or from earlier pagan times. The 5 wells are called Yewtree Well, Coffin Well, Hands Well, Hall Well and Town Well.

Figure 9 **Survey of a church – Tissington**

most substantial buildings, reflecting the craftsmanship of generations.

It is important for children to realize that many local churches have managed to survive the centuries because they were built and have been maintained with much care. As 'Houses of God' they projected His power and influence, which like the buildings themselves was timeless. This timelessness was confirmed in the services which the church offered. Babies came to it to be baptized, the young to be married, and the dead were brought to it to be buried. The tombs and memorials of the well-to-do within the church and the graves of the poor outside served as continual reminders that Christianity spanned the centuries.

Using the church building as a starting-point, how could a study be developed? The questions asked might concentrate the children's attention upon one specific aspect of the building (e.g. stained-glass, tombs, brasses, parish registers) or seek to set the church within a much broader framework (e.g. changes in architectural styles, the local history of the parish). The following indicates possible approaches.

Looking outside

The ground-plan

Whenever possible, children should be provided with a simple plan of the building. This will help to ensure that even the least confident have a 'map' on which to plot their own discoveries. When the children have visited a number of churches (and discovered in the process the essential features of church architecture), they should be encouraged to make their own plan on centimetre-squared cartridge paper.

Construction

What materials have been used for the walls and the roof? Has more than one type of material been used for the walls (e.g. stone and flint; flint, tile scrapes; wood; or brick)?

External features

Has the church a *tower or spire*? Is the tower square, round, octagonal, or triangular? Round towers are to be found mainly in Norfolk and Suffolk, where there is a shortage of stone for building. Many of these round towers are older than the church itself, dating from the tenth century and earlier. They are thought by archaeologists to have marked watercourses and waterways. East Anglian legend has it that round towers were 'water casings left bare when Noah's Flood subsided'.

Is there a *weather vane*? The fish, the symbol of the early Christians;* the crossed keys, the symbol of St Peter (Matthew 16: 19); and the cockerel (Matthew 26: 69–75) are the designs most commonly used.

Are there *gargoyles* around the guttering? A gargoyle is a decorated waterspout which takes rain-water from the roof. They are often carved to represent dragons and demons, pointing to the fact that even after Christianity had become widespread, primitive religious beliefs continued to be held. The fiercer the gargoyle, the less likely was it that evil spirits would haunt the churchyard. Children could be invited to note where the gargoyles are placed. Are they spread evenly around the building or are there more on the north side? The north side of the churchyard was for a long period in history regarded as that 'place of darkness' (i.e. the place that the sun did not touch). This explains why the south aisle of most churches pre-dates the north aisle, and why the south side of a churchyard was more popular for burial than was the north.

Is there a *public clock*? For a long period in our history the church clock (and its bells) kept time for the great majority of parishioners. The clock will be particularly worth studying if it has an unusual face (e.g. showing the phases of the moon) or have 'jacks' (dolls which strike the time).

Although sundials are sometimes found on church towers or in the churchyard, scratch dials are much more common. A scratch dial also uses shadow-fall to indicate the passage of time. The scratch dial was always cut into a south-facing wall, usually near the doorway or porch. It takes the form of a rough circle, usually divided into segments 15° apart, radiating from a shallow hole at the centre. This hole might once have held a metal gnomon (rod) which cast a shadow across the circular dial. More probably, the hole was for centring a wooden stick which the passer-by would have to find. A classroom study of ways of measuring time might seem an unlikely consequence of visiting a church. However, the making of accurate shadow clocks is an activity appropriate to children across the whole primary age range.

Is there a *lich-gate*? 'Lich' or 'lych' is the Saxon word for 'corpse'. Literally the lich-gate is the 'gate of the dead'. It once played an important part in the funeral service. The body, placed on a wheeled cart, was taken to the gate to await the priest. Only in recent times

---

* The initial letters of the Greek words for Jesus Christ, Son of God spell out the Greek word for 'fish'.

have the dead been buried in coffins. For a long period of our history the law required that the dead be buried in a woollen shroud. The wool of the shroud gave protection to the corpse from the worst of the weather.

Are there *yew trees* in the churchyard? Yew trees were sacred in pre-Christian Britain. It was the custom in Mediterranean countries to plant evergreen trees in graveyards and the practice may therefore have been brought to Britain by priests trained in Rome. Edward I (1272–1307) ordered that yew trees be planted around churches to give protection against the weather. Since yew wood was also essential for making bows for archers, it may be that his concern for the church was influenced by considerations of defence.

Inscriptions, dates, and carvings on tombs can be recorded by taking rubbings (see page 28). To which saint is the church *dedicated*? The most popular dedication is to St Mary. However, it is the more unusual dedications which provide opportunities for research. We could classify dedications as follows:

1. Biblical, New Testament apostles (e.g. St Michael, St Paul, and St Peter.
2. Historical figures (e.g. St Margaret of Scotland, St Chad, St Felix, St Cuthbert, St David, and St Germanus).
3. Legendary figures (e.g. St George and St Christopher).
4. Local saints (e.g. St Adhelm in Dorset, Gloucestershire, and Wiltshire; St Edmund in Suffolk; and St Swithin at Winchester).
5. Saints associated with particular crafts, professions, and callings (e.g. churches dedicated to St Nicholas, patron saint of sailors, are often near the sea); others in this category include St Crispin (boot-makers), St Giles (hospitals), and St Tibba (falconers).

This still leaves opportunity for a great deal of local research. There are parish churches dedicated to St Wendreda, St Morwenna, St Mary de Haura, St Wilfred, St Beuna, St Wulfram, St Nectan, St Hardulph, St Cressian, St Protus, St Hyacinth, St Candida, St Wystan, St Ronald, and St Uncumba. The majority of these have particular local associations, and it is always worthwhile to look in the area for further evidence – e.g. a holy well (the well of St Neot at St Neot, Cornwall). Are there other nearby churches with similar dedications or windows depicting the saint during his or her life? Some churches have no dedication. This is usually because they were brought into use during the Commonwealth.

Are there any interesting *tombs or memorials* in the churchyard? The inscriptions on gravestones often contain a great deal of information about local families and local occupations and trades. This might

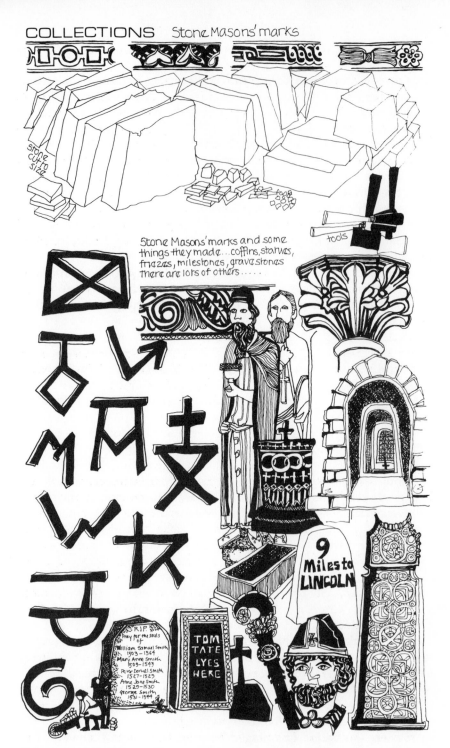

Stone Masons' marks and some
things they made...coffins, statues,
friezes, milestones, gravestones
There are lots of others.....

stone
cut to
size

tools

9
Miles to
LINCOLN

RIP
Pray for the souls
of
William Samuel Smith
1503-1564
Mary Anne Smith
1505-1543
Peter Daniel Smith
1527-1529
Anne Jane Smith
1529-1530
George Smith
1531-1549

TOM
TATE
LYES
HERE

Figure 10 Collections – Stone mason. Many old buildings contain the personal signature of the masons who worked on them.

prompt research into whether any descendants of these families still live in the parish and whether the trades and occupations continue to be practised. In addition, gravestones often record unusual occurrences (e.g. struck dead by lightening) and the contribution made to the community by the deceased during his or her lifetime.

Tomb sculpture is invariably rich in symbolism – e.g. the hourglass, the scyth, the skull. From this somewhat morbid starting-point children could be invited to make a collection of contemporary symbols. Where do we use symbols rather than words? Why?

Life expectancy in earlier periods of history can also be explored through inscriptions. Using the statistics which they collect, children can be encouraged to compare the life expectancy of men who died between 1750 and 1800, 1800 and 1850, 1850 and 1900, and 1900 and 1950. Similar figures could be obtained for women. What is life expectancy today? A parallel survey could focus upon infant and child mortality.

Is there a *porch*? In medieval times the porch was the centre of parish administration. It continues to be a place through which information is disseminated (e.g. local authority elections). Often it was a place where equipment was kept – like buckets and thatch hooks for fire-fighting, and the mort-safe (where corpses were kept safe before burial).

Looking inside

Study of a topic brings with it the need to master specialist terms. Therefore, it follows that when the church is used as a starting-point for environmental studies, children will need to be helped to understand a 'new' language. Some of the words and phrases they will meet will be comparatively easy to master (e.g. 'font', 'aisle', 'nave', 'chapel'); others will be far more complex (e.g. 'sedilia', 'piscina', 'rood-screen'). When children have had some experience of using church buildings as an entry point to environmental studies, these more complicated phrases (and the practices and ideas to which they relate) can be examined.

When taking groups of children into a church, I have invariably found it useful to begin the visit with a few moments of quiet sitting and looking. This not only encourages children to use their eyes, it also allows them to respond to atmosphere. A brief reminder of things to look for can be followed by individual exploration, note-taking, drawing, rubbing, and photography.

Children should be encouraged to look beyond the obvious – to decorations (billet, chevron, cable, dog-tooth, table), roof bosses, corbels, gargoyles, windows, and vaulting. Individually children

Chart 4

Glossary of 'ecclesiastical architecture' terms

Aisle	Part of church, on either side of nave or chancel
Apse	Recess at the end of a building – usually semicircular
Boss	A decoration at the junction of two or more ribs of a vault
Chancel	Eastern part of church
Chantry (chapel)	Chapel set aside for regular masses for specific person or persons
Clerestory	The side of wall of the nave above the aisle roof, usually pierced with windows
Credence (table)	A table for holding the vessels of the mass
Crossing	The space where the east–west axis of the church is crossed
Gargoyle	Stone waterspout by the north–south transepts
Misericords	Hinged wooden seats, usually found in the choir
Nave	Main body of church
Piscina	A small hand-basin with a drain beside an altar. Used to cleanse sacramental vessels
Pyx	Above the medieval altar was often a canopy. From this hung a box containing the Sacrament for administration to the sick and dying
Reredos	Ornamental screen at the back of altar
Sedilia	Seats for officiating clergy carved into the south wall of the sanctuary
Squints	Holes pierced through the wall on one or both sides of the chancel arch to give sight of the high altar; also known as 'hagioscopes'
Transept	Transverse part of a cruciform church set at right-angles to the east–west axis
Tympanum	The filling of the arch of a Norman doorway; in classical architecture, the triangular space enclosed by the sides of a pediment
Water stoup	A recessed basin near the porch for holding holy water

could be invited to look for particular things and report to the group on their findings. Windows and bosses are particularly interesting topics, which will repay detailed study as they often feature local legends, commemorate events, or record (through coats of arms and heraldic devices) the church's association with powerful benefactors and with royalty. Certain aspects are particularly worthy of study, as follows.

Church furniture. This covers a whole range of items: e.g. the carving on pews, pew-ends, and choirstalls often offers evidence of life in times past; fonts, their design and decoration; and embroidery (on altar frontals and on kneelers and banners).

Written records. Most old churches can boast continuous records dating back to the regulations of Henry VIII's Vicar-General, in 1538, which required that every parish priest should keep a register of christenings, weddings, and burials. Though difficult for young children to follow, lists can still be impressive. The registers at All-Hallows-by-the-Tower, in the City of London, for example, clearly show how deaths increased during the summer of 1665, the year of the Great Plague.

Memorials. Effigies of people provide perhaps the best reason for using the church as a starting-point for environmental studies. The effigies represent people who lived, married, raised families, went to war, and left bequests for the poor, and, in fact, died in and around the very place that the children themselves are studying. Though dead, they somehow bring the past to life, illustrating changes of fashion over the centuries – in dress, armour, hairstyle, and ornament – more effectively than a history book. The tombs themselves also reflect changes in taste and fashion, developing from the flat twelfth-century slab to the sophisticated grandeur of the richly coloured, life-size figures (with canopy, armorial bearings, and family motto) of Stuart days. After the grotesquely dressed statues used to commemorate politicians, soldiers, and explorers of the nineteenth century, fashion has now turned full-circle and we share, once more, the simpler tastes of the Plantagenets. When using tombs as the basis for study, it is important to remind the children that it was only the rich who were buried inside the church, ordinary folk were buried in the churchyard.

Effigies on tombs also comment upon the changing nature of religious belief. Throughout the Middle Ages it was believed that at the Resurrection all the dead would come before God's judgment. Therefore, it was important to portray the dead at the height of their powers. Thus a person who died aged 80 was often portrayed as being only 30.

The materials used for tombs are also worth noting. Those carved in stone are the most common, and often they are richly decorated in gold leaf or brightly enamelled. When the Puritans under Oliver Cromwell held power (1649–60), many tombs were damaged or destroyed on the grounds that it was wrong to have statues in the House of God. Tombs made of wood, marble, alabaster, and bronze are also to be found.

Wall paintings. These are still to be found in some churches. They serve to remind children of a time when few people could read. Paintings (and stained-glass) were a useful means of illustrating biblical texts and of underlining the Christian message.

Collections. Has the Church a museum or collection of documents which give further evidence of the growth and development of the community it was built to serve? This is a far-ranging question which in some cases will result in little, but in others provides source material for a year's work. As one might expect, the most comprehensive collections are in the bigger churches (those at Westminster Abbey and Durham Cathedral being particularly extensive). Many churches have indentures and old seals, and chained Bibles are surprisingly common.

Extending the study

Cathedrals and monastic foundations

Provided that the children have made some study of their local church, they should have no difficulty in understanding that a cathedral is, essentially, the parish church writ large. Architecturally it has been designed for the same purpose (i.e. the observance of religious rites), and one should expect to find certain similarities.

There are, however, certain points which need to be made. The cathedral is the seat of the bishop of the diocese – and so all cathedrals have a bishop's throne. Moreover, since many of our cathedrals were built long before the Reformation, they often contain traces of the monastic foundations from which they evolved. Thus there might be a Chapter House (that at Wells is superb), cloisters (those at Gloucester boast both a lavatorium where the monks washed and the recess in which they hung their towels), or other outbuildings (at Peterborough these include the Abbot's and Prior's lodgings and a number of gateways, and at Ely there is the sacristy and almonry as well as a fourteenth-century barn).

During the visit it might be necessary to introduce a few more architectural terms. Chantry chapels, for example, can be seen in many parish churches, but for sheer quantity we need to go to the medieval foundations of Canterbury, York, Lichfield, Worcester, Salisbury, Winchester, or Norwich. It is also more likely that these great churches will have undercrofts or crypts. The atmosphere evoked by the claustrophobic dimness of Rochester is in strange contrast with the airy lightness of Wren's St Paul's.

It might also prove of worth to try to link the cathedral with its immediate surroundings, particularly where the town has historical significance. A town in the Middle Ages was often based upon a very simple planning formula – 'a square for God and a square for Man'. Thus ecclesiastic and commercial interest could live side by side without undue friction, both groups being protected by the city wall and perhaps a castle. Do street names suggest that, in the past, certain areas enjoyed ecclesiastic patronage (e.g. Crucifix Lane, Abbey Walk, Monastery Street, Bishops Place), while others were more devoted to trade and commerce (e.g. Madder Market, Exchange Street, Cornhill)?

The cathedrals at Coventry, Liverpool, and Guildford could be looked at from quite a different viewpoint, particularly if the children are of upper junior or middle school age. In these modern buildings attempts have been made to relate the Christian message to present-day society, contemporary artists, designers, and craftsmen employing contemporary techniques to modern materials. One has only to think of the impressive west window of Coventry with its etched angels, or the great circular lantern of the Roman Catholic Cathedral of Christ the King in Liverpool, to appreciate how effectively this philosophy is being applied.

Abbeys, monasteries, and priories

The majority of our cathedrals can trace their history back to pre-Reformation times, and it is therefore advisable to give children the opportunity of visiting at least one of them before attempting to interest the group in the many abbey ruins which dot the country-side. The cathedral building should give an idea of the skills of the medieval craftsmen – difficult to grasp when looking at sad (though well-kept) piles of fallen masonry.

It would also be helpful if some picture could be built up of the life of the monks and nuns. For this, the following information will prove of use. All the various foundations may be described as 'religious houses': a house of monks was called a monastery, that of nuns a nunnery. A monastery or nunnery was designated an abbey where an abbot or abbess was a resident member of the community; otherwise the religious house was known as a priory (under a prior or prioress). In this case, it was usually an offshoot from an abbey and dependent upon it. In addition to these, the houses of the itinerant friars were usually called friaries and those of the Carthusian monks were known as Charterhouses.

Personally, I do not consider it necessary to dwell on the particular differences between the orders, except to stress that the friars were wanderers and to mention that the Carthusians did not follow the typical monastic day since (apart from certain communal meals and services) they prayed, ate, and slept in solitude. Dress varied of course from one order to another, but again the task of the teacher is not to fill up each child with tedious details, but rather to make a particular way of life come alive. A brief description of the habit (with colour variations) should suffice, though this allows children with particular interest in costume to follow a study of their own, supporting written work with appliqué pictures, felt collages, or dressed dolls.

It is impossible to state exactly how the monk spent his day. This would vary according to the order and each house would have individual peculiarities. Moreover feast days and other holy days required particular observances; however, children are usually impressed with the following basic timetable:

2.30 a.m.	Rise, psalms and prayers
	Nocturn (the first service)
	Matins
Dawn	Prime
	Reading in the cloister
	Ablutions
8.00 a.m.	Terce
	Morrow mass
9.00 a.m.	Meeting in the Chapter House (to plan day-to-day life of the monastery)
10.00 a.m.	Reading
	Work
Noon	Sext
	High mass
	Nones
2.00 p.m.	Meal in the refectory or frater (often eaten in silence, a brother reading from the scriptures or Church Fathers)
	Reading
	Work
5.00 p.m.	Vespers
	Light refreshment
6.00 p.m.	Compline
7.00 p.m.	Retire to the dorter to sleep

The work which the monks and nuns would follow was very varied. Apart from the Cistercian houses, servants performed most of the manual tasks, giving the religious the opportunity to concentrate on activities requiring a greater degree of skill – teaching the novices, illuminating the scriptures, keeping the abbey records and accounts, carving, painting, tending the sick, preparing the music, and indeed everything which had to be done to ensure that a large community lived together happily, from buying food and wine, mending the towels and bed covers to the supply, at three-weekly intervals, of hot water for head shaving.

A school visit to an abbey ruin or to a large cathedral will require a considerable amount of preparation. My experience would suggest that it is, however, worthwhile. Once the pattern of life, within the

Chart 5

Abbey officials

Abbot	Superior of abbey or monastery, elected by the monks themselves. The Prior was the Abbot's deputy, and the Sub-prior the Prior's assistant
Almoner	Official with care of the local poor
Cellarer	In charge of stores, food, wine, ale
Chamberlain	In charge of monks' sleeping quarters, clothing, and footwear
Fraterer	In charge of the dining-room, the lavatorium
Hospitaller	Provider of hospitality for guests
Infirmarian	In charge of hospital
Kitchener	In charge of kitchens
Novice-master	Charged with education of novitiates (young monks)
Precentor	Director of church services and music
Refectorian	In charge of the refectory and its furnishings
Sacristan	Keeper of vestments, church plate
Succentor	Assistant to the Precentor

pattern of a building, has been understood, the children can quickly relate particular functions to particular parts of the ground-plan. Arches, pillars, arcades, fallen corbels, and bosses provide inspiration for drawing. Occasionally the visit can spark off all manner of follow-up work. The Abbot's Kitchen at Glastonbury, for example, with its brilliantly conceived roof built to allow the air to circulate freely, led to a long discussion with one group of 10-year-olds on the properties of heat. The same class contained several children who had heard of King Arthur. At Glastonbury legend has it that Arthur is buried with his queen – myth, romance, fiction, or fact? As teachers, part of our task should be to make children aware that fact and fiction, romance, and legend have sometimes to be unravelled if we are really to understand the past.

Readings from literature can be used to deepen still further children's interests. While we ought to include legends like those of St Patrick and St David, children should also be exposed to extracts from Bede (*Ecclesiastical History of the English Nation*), Chaucer (*Canterbury Tales*), and St Francis (*The Little Flowers of St Francis*). Records and tapes of plainsong chant are also widely available, and the occasional short extract can do much to evoke the spirit of a long gone age.

When making a local survey, it is important that children are encouraged to list other places of worship in the area. Some will be Christian (Roman Catholic church, Quaker meeting-house, Baptist chapel, Salvationist gospel hall), and others will be places where

Contemporary buildings point to the changing nature of British society

people practise faiths more recently introduced to Britain.

Christianity first came to Britain when it was part of the Roman Empire. As a consequence, the Christian faith has had over 1600 years in which to become rooted in all aspects of life, in ways of thinking, in attitudes, and in custom and folklore. Christian beliefs have coloured our laws, influenced such diverse entities as education and architecture, and helped shape our system of government. The impact of Christianity can be seen throughout the year across the countryside: wells are dressed, parish boundaries are 'beaten', ploughs are dedicated, and the harvest received by priests who continue traditions stretching back deep into our rural past. Now the vicar may be more educated than his medieval or Norman counter-part, but it is well to remember that the lives of all three proclaim the teaching of a mystical God who lived and died in Asia Minor.

In the years since the Second World War the religious 'map' of Britain has changed. Although Christianity remains the religion of the state and (in theory) the religion of the bulk of the population, immigrant peoples from Africa and Asia have introduced a new religious dimension to Britain. Religious diversity is no longer represented by Christian sects (Quaker, United Reform, Catholic), but in fundamental differences of belief and practice.

This book seeks to examine the interaction of people and the landscape and the way in which the shape of buildings and towns comment upon historical change. The mosque to be found in Bradford or East London is as much a reflection of the historical development of the nation as the parish church or the abbey ruin, the pagoda in a city park as significant a pointer to a way of thinking as a cathedral spire.

The very immediacy of changes like these provides exciting opportunity for teachers who work in areas where settlement from abroad has brought in its wake religions new to Britain. The opportunity needs to be seized. The buildings themselves will offer a starting-point for enquiry. How many different kinds of religious building are to be found within walking distance of school? How are these buildings used? What is particular about their design? How are they decorated? How does a mosque differ from a church? What do the people who worship there believe?

This approach can be supported by drawing upon the willingness of local religious leaders to explore their faith with others. I would recommend that the initial approach be on a personal level. Informal links, established between local religious leaders and the school can provide an invaluable means of bringing children to understand the diversity of religious beliefs now to be found in Britain. To suggest that this area is one which is best left to the initiatives of individual teachers is not to dodge the issue. Teachers need to look at the social and cultural composition of the community in which they work, and as a consequence of so doing, plan links which are appropriate to their children. Furthermore, the view that children should be taught about religions other than Christianity within a Religious Education framework is one to which I would whole-heartedly subscribe. It is not one which needs to be explored in detail in this book.

Throughout all the work in this area one central point needs to be stressed. Down the centuries, Britain has allowed people from other lands to settle, bringing with them their own culture and customs. (Evidence of this can be found in many towns, e.g. the 'Dutch' quarter of Colchester.) The more recent immigrants are but part of a continual movement of peoples which has gone on since prehistory. Our task as teachers is to equip children with an understanding of this and of the multi-faceted society which has thereby been created. This curriculum consideration applies whether we teach in Bradford or Tonbridge Wells, Slough or Cheltenham. Indeed it may well be that it is in those areas in which the established church continues unchallenged that the greatest effort must be made to emphasize that the parish church (which may have stood for centuries) is but one aspect of a religious dimension that has been sought by men and women since the dawn of time.

6 Places of defence

Hardly a day passes without some reference to defence being made in the press or on television. It might be a comment on the latest round of international arms talks, a feature on spring manoeuvres in the Baltic, or a discussion centred on a recent nuclear test.

Turn the pages of any large-scale road atlas of Britain, and almost every one will contain some hint of this deep-seated concern for safety and protection. Every castle ruin, hill fort, earthwork, dyke, medieval city wall, disused airstrip, coastal look-out, Tudor beacon, and nineteenth-century Martello tower comments upon a human preoccupation – the need, in time of trouble, to feel 'safe'. To this extent a common concern links in time the builders of Maiden Castle (Dorset) with the scientists who fashion modern military technology. It is a concern for survival and protection against 'enemies', who are not the members of a particular 'tribe' or community.

Not all of this preoccupation will be found on maps. Neglected and overgrown pill-boxes of the Second World War, quiet stretches of waterfront where once men-of-war were built (like Buckler's Hard, Hampshire), and listening-stations on deserted moorland all serve as reminders of the tensions which have divided, and continue to divide, peoples and nations.

In exploring any theme, and here one which centres on places of defence is no exception, an essential part of the teacher's task is to provoke discussion. What can be learnt about the past from this place? Why was this site chosen? What does it tell us about the people who constructed it? How might it have looked when it was being used? What materials were used in its construction? Where did

In many border areas (England/Wales; England/Scotland) houses were fortified. This house (Markenfield, Ripon, Yorkshire), built in the early 1300s, was surrounded with high walls and a moat and protected by a gatehouse and a drawbridge

they come from? Today is the site still used for the purpose for which it was originally intended? What circumstances may have led to a change in its function or to its falling into disuse?

These kinds of question could be put to children of primary age when they are visiting a castle, or as they record the position of concrete pill-boxes in the fields of a rural village. Simple deduction will suggest some answers, but many of the questions deserve a deeper response. It may be that some children will be led to question the need which human beings have to 'protect their own space'. Here I am not suggesting that the issues of peace and war should play a dominant part in the school curriculum. What is important, however, is that children be given a historical framework within which they can set and examine such issues.

I have already indicated that local enquiry is the most satisfactory way of developing the skills necessary for environmental research. The very fact that a site *is* local means that it can be continually re-visited and investigated over time. For this to be possible, teachers need to come to know in considerable detail the area immediately around their school and be able to establish general principles from a study of specific local examples. Thus a study of defence for a class in a South Coast town might begin by an examination of the way in which military engineers had built gun emplacements and watch-towers into a stretch of cliff face. Although the children in a Dorset village (approaching the topic through an analysis of a Bronze Age hill fort) and those in Beaumaris (using an Edwardian castle) begin from very different starting-points, certain central questions will be common to them all. When and why was this site chosen? What evidence is there that this site was built to give defence? Are there any clues which we can 'read' from its shape, position, and construction? Why was it necessary?

The use of local sites to teach children the skills of observing, questioning, and recording, as well as imagining, will mean that they are more likely to respond to whole-day excursions to places beyond the school's immediate neighbourhood.

Having indicated that 'defence' is reflected in many different ways (from hill fort to gun emplacement), let me now outline some approaches through a study of fortifications. Inevitably such a study is likely to be concerned with some of the medieval castles which are to be found across Britain. Such buildings (whether they are romantic ruins like Bodiam, in Sussex, and Richmond, Yorkshire, or stately homes like Warwick and Berkeley, in Gloucestershire) appeal to children – perhaps this is because a combination of stories and legends, television serials, and picture-book illustrations have combined to create a haunting impression of castle life. Drawing upon this interest, it is possible to encourage children to question some of these romantic assumptions and begin to look at the past with rather more honesty.

It is for these reasons that many of the areas of study which are suggested in the pages which follow are directly linked to the medieval period. Nevertheless, the questions posed are equally relevant to hill fort and coastal emplacement.

The first questions which need to be asked centre on the people who built the fortification being visited: when did they live? How did they dress? Why did they choose this particular site? What materials were used? When was the fortification last used? The answers to such questions will immediately give some insight into the way a study might develop. Since the answers which result from these initial questions can have deeper implications, let us examine them in a little greater depth.

(a) *How old is the site*? This question will need to be phrased in such a way as to be pertinent to the children concerned in the study. Portchester (Hampshire), for example, is essentially Roman with considerable medieval additions; Kenilworth (Warwickshire) dates from 1155 but its link with Elizabeth I and the masques which were held during her reign in John of Gaunt's 'new' buildings will interest children far more than an analysis of architectural terms; and Chiddingston (Kent) is hardly a castle at all, being a house in 'castle style' which incorporates some medieval features. In other words, we should be specific in our initial aim – most castle sites span the centuries and present far too much material for children to grasp on one visit.

(b) *Why was the site chosen*? Castles were built for a variety of reasons, most of which even young children can appreciate: first, to guard a pass, river valley, a shore, or a river-crossing – e.g. Dolwyddelan Castle, Gwynedd; Deal Castle, Kent; Tilbury fort, Essex; and Martello towers (South Coast).

Secondly, castles were built to administer and control an area – e.g. Caernarvon Castle, the Tower of London. In this connection, older children might like to plot all the castles built during a particular period of history. The Edwardian castles of Wales are then seen as part of a far-seeing plan to subjugate the Welsh. On the other hand, a castle sited like the one at Corfe (Dorset) merely controls a stretch of land (in this case, the Isle of Purbeck) and little else.

Thirdly, castles provided a refuge. This was a prime function of all fortifications and defence works. In this respect, Maiden Castle (Dorset), a pre-Roman hill town, was meeting the same need as the medieval castles at Berwick, Edinburgh, and Borthwick. Church towers were sometimes used as places of refuge (e.g. St Mary's, Swanage), as were houses (e.g. the Vicar's House, Corbridge, Northumberland; and Ightham Mote, Kent). Children could be encouraged to compare this function of castles and fortifications with that of the concrete pill-boxes of the Second World War. These were designed to give protection to selected defenders against attack from enemies coming from across the sea by ship and by air. Therefore they protected the civilian population only indirectly – unlike Maiden Castle, for example, whose earth walls could give protection to the whole of the local population and their moveable possessions as well as the domestic animals.

(c) *What materials have been used for building*? The earliest Norman castles were built of wood – an earthwork, surrounded by a moat, crowned with a palisade enclosing a wood tower. Indeed it is worth noting that castles were first introduced into Britain by the Normans and have been defined by B.S. St J. O'Neil, sometime Chief Inspector of Ancient Monuments to the Ministry of Public Buildings and Works, as 'a private fortress of a king or noble constructed of earth or stone erected after the Norman Conquest'.

Adjoining the wooden or stone tower (the 'donjon' or safe place of refuge) was a banked and walled courtyard. In this (the bailey), household buildings were erected. The great majority of the early Norman castles were built of wood and were replaced in the years following the Conquest with castles of stone. Nevertheless, the initial earthworks are still visible and are worth exploring. Examples of this type of earthwork are quite common throughout England and the border countries. Particularly fine examples are to be seen at Berkhamsted (Hertfordshire), Bolingbroke (Lincolnshire), Pickering (Yorkshire), Lewes (Sussex), Castle Rising (Norfolk), Castle Headingham (Essex), and Rochester (Kent). The stone castles which developed from these primitive motte and bailey strongholds were of several types. The keep, for example, was built in stone at Colchester, and in London during the reign of William the Conqueror (d. 1087) and some stone curtain (protecting) walls (e.g. as at Richmond, Yorkshire) date from a similar period.

The materials used for castle building were often quarried locally, although some were brought from far afield (e.g. stone from Caen was used for the White Tower, London). Looking at the stone is worthwhile. Castles aren't just a uniform, dull grey, a fact that most illustrators of children's history books seem to ignore. Berkeley castle (Gloucestershire) is pink, Rougemont (Exeter) is rich red, Ashby-de-la-Zouch (Leicestershire) is rich brown, and Corfe (Dorset) is white. The stones reflect the resources of the locality, and it might prove profitable to encourage children to list places where similar materials have been used (e.g. the church; the parish dovecot; or cottages, often incorporating dressed stones removed from castles which were razed during the Civil War).

Brick was incorporated into some castles during the later Middle Ages, though as this period also marks the advent of gun-powder we could regard these buildings as little more than the final flowerings of a dying age. The keep at Tattershall (Lincolnshire), for example, has an abundance of defensive paraphernalia, its purpose being to show how important a person the owner was rather than to defeat an encamping army. Other famous brick-built castles may be seen at Hurstmonceux (Sussex) and Kirby Muxloe (Leicestershire).

(d) *How did castles develop?* Children need to be helped to realize that life during any period of history is not static. A cursory study of the development of, say, cars over the past twenty-five years will serve to indicate the relationship between ever changing design and new technology. This relationship is equally pertinent to the evolution of historical artefacts. The changing design of castles and fortifications comment upon new knowledge and heightened skill as well as the technology which led to an evolution in the methods of warfare.

As we have seen, the first castles were based upon the idea of a central 'donjon' or keep. This was given greater protection by throwing a wall around it, and by separating the walls from the surrounding land by digging a ditch or moat. It follows on from this that the keep was the stronghold, and that the most likely place of unauthorized entry was through the gatehouse. Thus defence of the gatehouse became a priority – with portcullis, drawbridge, and watch-towers.

The realization that the gatehouse was the first (and possibly final) line of defence led military architects to question the need for a central keep. The *keep gatehouses* which they designed concentrated defence around the castle entrance. Sometimes, as at Caerlaverock, Dumfries, the gatehouse lay at the apex of a triangle formed by three high curtain walls. Sometimes, as at Rhuddlan, North Wales, defence was centred on two keep gatehouses, one on each side of a diamond-shaped walled bailey.

Another commonly adopted method was to throw a great circular wall around the site chosen for the castle. Along this wall towers were built. Each tower was connected to its neighbour through a corridor built into the wall itself. There were few entrances at ground level, and since each tower could be shut off from its neighbour, each became in time of siege an individual keep. Castles of this type (e.g. Framlingham, Suffolk) are known as 'castles of encientre'.

The Crusades had a tremendous effect upon castle development: military architects learned from the battles with the Turks that castles could have defences at two levels and that round towers were to be preferred over square towers. These were stronger, less expensive in materials, and easier to defend (having no dead ground below them). Edward I's architect, Master James of St George, built a castle at Beaumaris (Anglesey) which incorporates all of these ideas. It has two gatehouses and all of the inner ring of towers were constructed such that the defenders could fire over the heads of their fellows who were manning the outer walls. This fine example of a *concentric castle* marks the high point of castle building in Britain.

This brief summary is to provide a basic background to a study of medieval castles. It could be extended to show children how some of the principles implicit in castle architecture continued to be applied to defensive buildings erected in more recent periods of history – narrow slits through which weapons could be fired, the protection provided by thick walls, thoughtful planning of entrances and gateways, and external defences (a cliff face, trenches to make approach more difficult, or a watercourse).

A second approach is to examine the question why the castle became a military irrelevance. Gun-powder, first used in Europe at the battle of Crécy (1346) slowly changed the style of warfare. Henry VIII built castles to defend the channel coast (e.g. Deal, Walmer) but these were little more than gun emplacements.

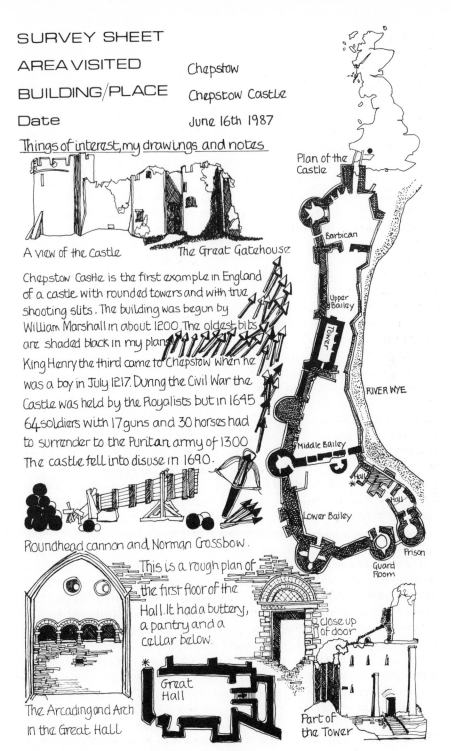

SURVEY SHEET

AREA VISITED   Chepstow

BUILDING/PLACE   Chepstow Castle

Date   June 16th 1987

Things of interest, my drawings and notes

Plan of the Castle

A view of the Castle   The Great Gatehouse

Chepstow Castle is the first example in England of a castle with rounded towers and with true shooting slits. The building was begun by William Marshall in about 1200. The oldest bits are shaded black in my plan. King Henry the third came to Chepstow when he was a boy in July 1217. During the Civil War the Castle was held by the Royalists but in 1645 64 soldiers with 17 guns and 30 horses had to surrender to the Puritan army of 1300 The castle fell into disuse in 1690.

Barbican

Upper Bailey

Tower

RIVER WYE

Middle Bailey

Hall

Hall

Lower Bailey

Prison

Guard Room

Roundhead cannon and Norman Crossbow.

This is a rough plan of the first floor of the Hall. It had a buttery, a pantry and a cellar below.

Great Hall

close up of door

The Arcading and Arch in the Great Hall

Part of the Tower

Figure 11 Survey of a castle – Chepstow

Chart 6

Glossary of terms: defence architecture

Allure	A wall-walk along a curtain wall
Ashlar	Dressed and cut stone
Bailey	The courtyard
Barbican	Gateway
Bartizan	Small turret built into the face of a curtain wall or tower
Bastion	Corner fortification
Corbels	Stone bracket for supporting a projecting battlement
Crenellations	Battlements on top of wall
Curtain	The wall enclosing the courtyard of the castle
Donjob	The keep
Embrasure	Open spaces in a crenellation through which archers shoot
Forebuilding	Outbuilding protecting entrance to keep
Garde-robe	A toilet
Gatehouse	Castle entrance
Keep	The donjon or safe place
Loophole	A slit in a wall for ventilation or for shooting through
Louver	An opening in the hall roof to let smoke escape from a central fire
Machicolation	Spaces (holes) left between corbels to enable defenders to throw down missiles upon attackers below

To some extent, the execution of Charles I (1649) can also be seen to mark the death of the castle. Many Royalist castles faced long sieges in the Civil War, and on surrender were usually 'slighted', so damaged that they could never again be used in war.

Exploring a castle with children can be dangerous and hair-raising! Assuming that there are two adults to 30 children, I have always found it wise to divide the group into two parties, each of which begins at a different part of the site. One adult can manage to lead 15 children over curtain walls and towers – but double the number, and the situation becomes unmanageable and positively dangerous.

Before the school visit, give the group some specific items to look for and make them aware of some of the basic architectural terms. While I am not convinced that an 8-year-old needs to know that a crenellated wall was broken into solids (merlons) and voids (embrasures) or that a parapet walk was called an 'allure', I *do* think that a teacher who is responsible for children of primary age needs to be aware of the sophistication of siege warfare (the workings of the drawbridge and portcullis, and the positioning of 'murder holes', or meutrieres, and oubliettes).

On a less sinister note, fireplaces, the Great Hall, and the kitchens provide a rich source of material for sketching. Most castles also had a chapel (which served to emphasize the closeness of church and

Mantlet	Defensive wall beyond the curtain wall
Merlons	The solid portions of a crenellation
Meurtriere	A 'murder hole' (usually found in an entrance passage)
Moat	An often water-filled ditch which ran around the castle
Motte	The earthen mound of an early castle
Newel	Staircase built round a central pillar
Obliette	A slit in the wall for ventilation or for shooting through
Portcullis	An iron or wood grating which could be dropped to block an entrance passage
Postern	Side-gate
Putlogs	Beams which supported a projecting timber gallery. Putlog holes are often found just below the crenellations on the keep
Rainures	Beams for raising a drawbridge
Sally port	A side-gate
Shell (keep)	A circular stone wall enclosing a donjon and courtyard
Undercroft	Store place
Ward	Courtyard enclosure of a castle

state during this period of our history).

In this connection, it is often worthwhile to visit the local church after visiting the castle, in order to see if there are any obvious links between the two buildings. Sometimes the church contains the funeral banners of a long dead local squire or the tombs of people who lived in the castle. If the tombs have effigies (e.g. as at Ashby-de-la-Zouch, Leicestershire), details of dress can be noted. Armorial bearings on pillars and roof bosses also provide material for subsequent research.

The castle walls are also worthy of study. How thick are they? What sort of windows (or 'loopholes') do they have? Is the window a simple slit or does it incorporate a round hole (an oilette)? Is the loophole in the form of a cross? Has the wall any gun-ports? Do castle walls join the town?

Also the human dimension of the castle can be emphasized. Using a prepared plan, children could be encouraged to mark elements which they find on the castle site which comment upon life within its walls. This could include methods of heating and lighting, water supply (why the well was of such importance), storage and preparation of food (buttery, undercroft, and kitchen), toilets ('garde-robe' or privy), ovens (one for bread, one for meat), a hall for the lord and his retainers, and a 'solar' to which the lord and his family could retire. Are there recesses cut into stone walls to form a cupboard (aumbry) or a wash-place (piscina)? On a less happy human note – is there a dungeon?

It is because castles have immediate appeal to young children that follow-up activities in the classroom can be so rewarding. Let me examine some of the possibilities in detail. Written work could be linked to the history of the castle, the children's descriptions being supported with their own pencil, pen, or pen-and-wash drawings. These 'guidebooks in miniature' appeal particularly to those members of the group who do not enjoy picture-making on a large scale. Stories about people who lived in the castle are often worth recording, and the fact that the incidents are macabre or bizarre seems to make it easier for children to retell them successfully. Here I am thinking of stories like the ghost of Henry VII, who returns to the drawing-room of Berkeley Castle to make sure that all the chairs face east, as they did in his day when the room was a chapel. Even sudden death – that of Edward II at Berkeley, of Richard II at Pontefract, and of Queen Mary at Fotheringhay – may seem less horrifying with the passage of time (though, personally, I would not dwell overlong on political blood-letting).

Some well-preserved castles have still an atmosphere of their own, which gifted children will be able to recapture in words – castles like Orford (Essex), whose very isolation conjures up ghostly images of horsemen hurrying across the marshes to the safety of its walls, or Castle Hedingham (Essex), nestling in a pretty valley, whose empty apartments lend themselves to fantasies of knights and their ladies at ease before the great fireplaces listening to the songs of some medieval troubadour.

Imaginative writing will also flow from events which children associate with castles – tournaments, feasts, soldiers on watch along the parapet walks, a visit of the king, or a sortie into the enemy's encampment – can inspire even the least verbally gifted child. If these sorts of activity are attempted, make sure that source pictures are available (weapons, clothing, furnishings, etc.).

English literature provides another source. For example, *Kenilworth* by Sir Walter Scott gives an over-romantic, anachronistic picture of castle life, but used with care it can do much to make history pictures come alive. Extracts may also be selected from the following works:

Anon. *Sir Gawain, Song of Roland*
Chaucer 'Knight's Prologue'
Sir Arthur Conan Doyle *The White Company, Sir Nigel*
Keats 'La Belle Dame sans Merci'
Anya Seton *Katherine*

Shakespeare Extracts from the historical plays (e.g. Henry V's speech before Harfleur)

Spenser *Faerie Queen*

Tennyson 'The Lady of Shalott'

J. R. R. Tolkien *The Lord of the Rings* (Part 3, Chapter X)

T. H. White *The Sword in the Stone*

Plans of a castle can also be made. These might be simple mathematical drawings or take the form of 'dimensional' maps. Children's books often contain end-papers drawn in this style, plans and elevations being liberally mixed.

The map/plan could be extended by including some of the surrounding countryside. If this is done, we come full-circle, for the castle was in fact built where it was for a reason, and involvement in plan-making may well help the least perceptive to grasp that fact.

While study of a medieval castle may provide the central focus of work with children, it is worthwhile to discover whether any other buildings in the locality have incorporated elements of castle architecture. The most obvious example is the church tower (which is often crenellated). There are likely to be many other examples – e.g. a railway complex with turrets and slit windows; a water-tower machicolated at roof level; a city gateway, the gatehouse beside an abbey or cathedral; the turreted walls of a medieval city; or a nineteenth-century folly. Street names also give clues to their preoccupation with safety and to town layout in medieval times – e.g. Old Bailey, Castle Square, Lower Curtain, Barbican, Sallyport Lane. Often the names remain long after the castle itself has disappeared.

7 Places of work

Much has been said in recent years of the need to relate what happens in schools to the world of work. Although such observations have been directed towards teachers in secondary schools, a study of the workplace can provide materials for an extensive topic for children of primary age.

The most appropriate starting-point is the area around the school. Today what kinds of work are available for men and women? Parents are understandably somewhat reticent in allowing their occupation (or lack of it) to feature in classroom work. Since it would be quite inappropriate to use parents' occupations as the basis of an enquiry, the easiest way is to obtain information through a mixture of direct observation and simple research.

The study could be approached by dividing the area around the school into four arbitrarily defined quadrants. Using a local street map, prepare a large-scale map of each section. The information which is to featured on the map is collected by the children (as a class or in groups) on short 'observation' and 'recording' walks. As each street and quadrant is covered a detailed picture will emerge as banks, offices, public houses, restaurants, garages, factories, public toilets, parking-sites, cinemas, bingo clubs, and public buildings (like police stations, fire stations, town hall, and custom-house) are noted and marked on the map. The older and more sophisticated the children are, the more complex the classification can be. For example, shops could be classified by the services which they offer to the public as well as by the products they sell, and factories and workshops could be grouped according to the industry of which they are a part.

Such a starting-point will provide much material for classwork: is industry concentrated in a particular area? Why are there more banks than hairdressers? Locally where do people go for entertainment? Why are there, perhaps, many factories making clothes or workshops repairing cars? Or why does the area have so few places of work? Or why are there so many hotels and restaurants? Additionally, is tourism an industry? How could one classify the work undertaken by the transport company whose terminus is close to the school? Why in a village might there be only one shop and two farms? What range of goods does the village shop carry? Is that range wider than one might expect to find in a town shop of similar size? How do the prices compare? Is the village store more expensive than the town shop, and if so, why might this be?

Much of the material acquired from local research can be presented through line and block graphs, Venn diagrams, pie-charts, and maps. It will also provide an opportunity to set city, town, and village within a broader context; this can be done by drawing upon the full range of Ordnance Survey maps currently available (1:50,000 series, 2 cm = 1 km; 1:10,000 series, 10 cm = 1 km; 1:2,500 series, 40 cm = 1 km). Obviously the larger the scale of the map, the more local detail that will be shown (including such things as quarry and mine workings, gravel pits, telephone boxes, post offices, and footpaths).

Children's direct observations can be supplemented with material extracted from Yellow Pages, local directories, and advertisement pages in local newspapers (job advertisements, local firms advertising their services. This simple local enquiry is also likely to reveal specific information about the area. For example, a number of firms may provide a service to a much larger enterprise. There would be no aviation support companies around Heathrow were the airport not there; few motor accessory plants in the Midlands had Birmingham not been the birthplace of the machine-tool industry (and therefore of cars); and fewer hotels and restaurants in, say, Scarborough had it not become a popular tourist resort with day-trippers after the arrival of the railway.

It may be that children will quickly grasp that the area that they are studying is closely identified with a particular industry. The closeness of such links may have been weakened in recent years but the evidence of the past remains to be uncovered – evidence of mining in the villages in Durham or South Wales; of shipbuilding in the Tyne; of locomotives in Swindon; of wool in Bradford, Halifax, and Huddersfield; and of cotton in Lancashire. This, in turn, might lead to an identification of the elements which combined to concentrate industries within particular areas of the country: for example, how Bristol, situated at a natural harbour on the west coast, was able to grow and flourish on a trade of slaves and tobacco; how Lancashire's fast-flowing streams not only powered the early mills, but also provided the soft water necessary for the processes of cleaning, dyeing, and bleaching the cotton upon which its prosperity came to depend; and how the proximity of iron and coal helped Coalbrookdale to become a centre of industrial innovation.

Inevitably such an analysis will introduce children to the pioneers of industrial change. Though I would not recommend that undue time be given to the technical nature of their discoveries, nevertheless children should be made aware of the people whose names are synonymous with the emergence of Britain as an industrial nation: for example, Thomas Newcomen, Matthew Boulton, James Watt, Richard Trevithick, George Stephenson (steam power); Abraham Derby and Henry Cort (iron); James Hargreaves, Richard Arkwright, Samuel Crompton, Edmund Cartwright (cotton); Josiah Spode and Josiah Wedgwood (ceramics); John Wilkinson (machine tools); Isambard Kingdom Brunel, Thomas Telford, and John McAdam (civil engineering); and Michael Faraday (electricity).

Some of these names have entered the language. Spode and Wedgwood describe a type of ceramic, Wilkinson is a famous trade mark, and macadam a type of road surface. Usage such as this, then, serves to indicate how words may form a bridge between past and present. For instance, surnames may hint at trades and occupations which were once common. Comments upon names such as Bowman, Butcher, Carpenter, Draper, Dyer, Farmer, Fletcher, Gardener, Mason, Miller, Potter, Smith, Tailor, Tanner, Turner, Weaver, Wright, etc. can provide the starting-point for a study of 'occupational' surnames currently on the school register (or on headstones in the local churchyard): what do these names mean? What did a fletcher make and why are there so very few following the trade today. If we were asked to invent surnames to fit contemporary jobs, which might they be?

Place names are also worth studying. For instance, place names beginning with 'O' often suggest a link with former iron workings (ore), as in Orgreave (Yorkshire), Orgrave (Lancashire), and Orsett (Essex). The ending '-hurst' is derived from the Saxon 'hyrst', meaning a thick wood, and is particularly associated with areas where iron was smelted with charcoal such as Ashurst (Hampshire), Wadhurst (East Sussex), and Lamberhurst (Kent). 'Staple'/'Stable' probably indicates some association with the manufacture or trade in wool, e.g. Barnstaple (Devon) and Dunstable (Bedfordshire).

Similarly, street names often point to how land was used in times past. Even today there are few old villages without a Mill Lane, and many have Iron Mill Path. Forge Way, Foundry Street, Colliery Walk,

Memorials in churches and burial grounds often comment upon industrial life. This memorial (Silkstone, Yorkshire) lists the names and ages of over twenty children who were killed in July 1834 while working underground in the local coalmine: Mary Sellors (aged 10), Elizabeth Clarkson (aged 11) and her brother, Sarah Jukes (aged 10) . . .

and Engine Road continue to exist long after the workplace which named them has been forgotten.

Children's understanding of the industry which is around them now can be deepened by inviting parents and grandparents to talk about the area as it was in their childhood: did people do the same work as they do now? In what ways has there been change? The changes which older people may focus on may be those things which the children themselves have noticed – e.g. an area of industrial dereliction, a pit no longer working, a factory closed, or advertisements painted on walls to proclaim companies which no longer exist.

Such an approach may be supported further by photographs. If the people who talk to the children can be encouraged to contribute old photographs of themselves and of their parents for incorporation into a classroom display, the study will be that much more enriched.

Chart 7

Examples of written sources

1662: 'To Woolwich to the ropeyard: there looked over the several sorts of hemp and did see the working and experiments of the strength and the change in the dressing of every sort.' (Samuel Pepys, 21 July)

1806: 'Our working hours were from 6 in the morning till 7 in the evening. We had 10 minutes to eat breakfast. Two days each week we had an hour allowed for dinner while the machines were oiled.' (a 13-year-old)

1830: 'The pit is very wet where I work and water comes over our clog tops. My clothes are wet through all day long.' (girl, commenting on work in coalmines)

1831: 'Wanted, in a Clergyman's family living quiet retired, a steady active person, a good plain cook. She will be requested to take a part of the house work and make herself generally useful.' (advertisement)

1851: 'One side of the lane is covered with old boots and shoes, old clothes, (men's and women's and children's) new lace for edgings and a variety of cheap prints and muslins: hats and bonnets: pots: tins: old knives and forks, old scissors: here and there a stall of American cheese, old glass, secondhand furniture. Mixed with these are a few china ornaments and toys.
'The prints and muslins are often heaped on the ground: where are also heaps of boots and shoes, piles of old clothes, hats and umbrellas. Some traders place their goods on stalls or over an old chair or clothes horse.' (Henry Mayhew, *London Labour and the London Poor*)

1866: A comment on non-industrial England:

> Forget six counties overhung with smoke
> Forget the snorting steam and piston stroke
> Forget the spreading of the hideous town.

(William Morris, *The Earthly Paradise*)

The use of photographs as a primary source of information is touched upon in almost every chapter of this book. Engravings, old prints, photographs from local newspapers, and postcards can be linked to extracts from the writings of people who knew the area in the past. Though long dead, their voices still speak, through diaries, letters, biographies, autobiographies, and novels.

The 'observational' walks in the streets immediately around the school (supported by the written and oral accounts, described above) will undoubtedly throw up a number of further areas of enquiry. There will be buildings (e.g. Mechanics' Institutes and libraries) which carry dedications and dates: street patterns (e.g. industrial housing with its back alleys, planned housing as in Robert Owen's New

1890: '. . . the woman's hands were busy with the matchboxes. Strips of magenta paper and thick pieces of wood came together with the help of a paste brush. They were then thrown on the ground to dry, forming pyramids of trays and lids which would presently be made into matchboxes tied up with string and sent back to factories which give 2¼d. per gross for match-boxes. Two little children stood on the floor amidst the trays and lids and an older boy chopped wood in a corner of the room with a look on his face of hungry impatience . . . The room had no furniture but the table, the bed, and a few old hampers; a heap of coke was near the fireplace with which to dry the woman's work, also some cabbage leaves and onion stalks. This refuse the chldren would eat later if nothing else was forthcoming. A dog would scarcely have swallowed it. But in these days animals are better off than slum children. (The owners of that attic has been heard to say: "My dog turns tail when I go in; it's so disgusting"). (Jack London, *People of the Abyss*)

The writings of Charles Dickens contain many vivid descriptions of life in Victorian Britain:

Fifty thousand lairs surrounded him where people lived so unwholesomely . . . Where inhabitants gasped for air. Through the heart of the town a deadly sewer ebbed and flowed in the place of a fine fresh river. (*Little Dorrit*, Chapter 3)

As he comes into the iron country . . . fresh green woods are left behind: and coal pits and ashes, high chimneys and red bricks, scorching fire and a heavy never lightening cloud of smoke becomes the feature of the scenery. (*Bleak House*, Chapter 63)

The hum of labour resounded from every house and the whirl of wheels and noise of machinery shook the trembling walls. The fires, whose lurid sullen light had been visible for miles blazed fiercely up in the great works and factories of the town. The din of hammers, the rushing of steam, the dead clanking of engines was the harsh music which arose from every quarter. (*The Pickwick Papers*, Chapter 50)

Lanark complex, garden cities like Welwyn, new towns like Milton Keynes, and medieval city centres like York and Norwich); statues to local benefactors; name boards and advertisements over working factories and derelict buildings; blocked and silted canals; narrow stretches of open land which once carried a railway track; Victorian brickwork on two sides of a road, hinting at a bridge and a railway which no longer exists; and a millpond and the remains of a millrace.

All of these elements indicate something of the work of the industrial archaeologist who seeks to find evidence of the methods used in times past to quarry and to mine, or to manufacture goods and to distribute them. A study which seeks to compare and contrast an area's contemporary industrial and commercial activity with that

Figure 12 Collections – carpenters marks. These were marks made by carpenters to identify beams and joints worked on in their workshops. The marks were used when assembling buildings on site.

which it enjoyed in the past does not mean that children need become trapped in the nineteenth century. The flint-mines of the Celts,* the merchant and craft guilds of the medieval period, the tide and wind mills of the seventeenth century, or the canals of the eighteenth century provide evidence of the drive and enterprise which has been characteristic of men and women since time began – the desire to improve the quality of life.

Children's understanding of the implications of industrial processes, and their awareness of the significance of particular discoveries and developments, is likely to be developed by simple direct observation and the use of printed material. Visits to working museums (e.g. Coalbrookdale, Shropshire, or Beamish, County Durham) and museums which are devoted to a particular occupation (e.g. tin-mining at Helston, Cornwall, or canal life at Stoke Bruerne, Northamptonshire),† and 'experiences' such as a journey on a steam train or a trip on a barge through the underground workings of a lead-mine, will do much to bring a study to life.

In this connection, it is worthwhile to try to enlist the support of specialist conservation groups in the area. Details of these can usually be obtained through the county library or museum service. While it may be impossible for young children to take an active part in their activity, some organizations have a junior section to which schools can affiliate.

To a large extent, the dramatic industrial and social changes of the past 200 years have been brought about by an increasing ability to master power. This fact offers an alternative approach to a study of our industrial past. Until steam provided 'the breath of new life', the only sources of power were those provide by people, animals, and wind and water. The theme of 'power' could include water and tide mills and be used to illustrate how relatively minor advances in technology and design can considerably improve efficiency. For example, the undershot water-mill, which in England dates from the twelfth-century, was much less efficient than the overshot wheel which was to replace it.‡ This improvement was significant when considered against the background of a largely agrarian economy. The mill was used for all manner of tasks – grinding corn, crushing stones, pulping fruit, raising water, and driving hammers in iron foundries. When industrialization came to the woollen industry, water was used to power the looms.

* For instance, Grimes Graves, Norfolk.
† The guidebook, *Museums and Galleries*, published annually by British Leisure Publications, contains an exhaustive list of specialist museums.
‡ In comparing the two types, Smeaton discovered that the overshot water-wheel gave over 40 per cent more power for the same water flow and wheel size.

Wind power was used whenever water power was not conveniently available. Although windmills were used for grinding corn, these were as often used to provide the power to the pumps which drained low-lying land. Like the watermill, the design of windmills developed and changed over time.

There are, broadly speaking, two kinds of windmill. The older post-mill is so called because its wooden frame was supported by a massive upright post which enabled it to be turned bodily into the wind. Chaucer's miller would certainly have worked in one of these mills, for it is the post-mill that we find pictured in contemporary carvings (e.g. in Bristol Cathedral). An improvement in mill design occurred in the late fourteenth century when a moveable top section was built on to the fixed frame. This meant that only the sails needed to be turned to face the wind. The earliest mills of this type were known as smock-mills and were built of wood (smock because in silhouette they resembled a man wearing a smock). The basic idea of the smock-mill, namely a revolving cap, was quickly incorporated into stone and brick buildings known as 'tower-mills'.

As a subject for picture-making, the English mill has perhaps attracted more than its fair share of attention from landscape artists. Children can also be encouraged to sketch in crayon or oil pastel. Remember, however, that each child need not draw the entire mill – by encouraging children to concentrate on particular aspects of the mill, a much better understanding of its form and structure will be obtained and this will be particularly valuable for follow-up work at school. Thus while some of the children draw the sails, the cap, or the fantail from various viewpoints, the rest of the group make simple silhouette drawings to show the overall shape of the mill.

In some parts of the country evidence of the windmill is not hard to find. William Cobbett in his *Rural Rides* counted 17 as he rode into Ipswich. The mills may no longer be working, and their sails may have disappeared, but the round brick or stone bases often remain. By recording the sites of local mills on an Ordnance Survey map of the area, children gain an insight into the importance they once enjoyed. Such a study might record, too, the differences in mill design; not all windmills have four sails or are constructed of brick; and the cap may be domed or gabled, conical or ogee-shaped, or even shaped like a boat. Even the grinding-stones merit research. Some were quarried in Derbyshire (Peak stone), but many were imported from France (Burr stones) and Germany (Cullen stones).

The theme of power could develop through a study of machinery driven by wind and water* to machinery powered by steam. The first steam-engine to be put to industrial use was Thomas Slavery's 'fire engine'. It was designed to pump water from the tin and copper mines of the West Country and patented in 1698. Thomas Newcomen's 'atmospheric engines' which appeared in 1712 were used extensively in coal, tin, lead, and iron mines and were an improvement of Slavery's design, but it took the combined skill of Watt, Boulton, Smeaton, and Trevithick to perfect the beam-engine.

Children who live in mining areas will find plentiful evidence of the old engine sheds (e.g. Stretham, Cambridgeshire; Nanty Mwyn, Dyfed; Glyn Pit, Glamorgan; Boscastle tin mine, Cornwall), and though many are rather gaunt and forbidding, they are well worth exploring by a small group. Beam-engines are to be seen in many industrial museums. If children are particularly interested in gaining better understanding of how the machines worked, they could hardly do better than make models from a plastic kit, available from hobbies shops.

Just as the coal-driven steam-engine meant that factories and mills need no longer hug the valley bottom, but could be built wherever raw materials were most conveniently situated, the development of gas and electricity and the harnessing of oil has meant that power can now be taken wherever it is required. The siting of a factory is no longer dependent upon convenient proximity to a coalfield or to a river, canal, or railway line along which a bulky source of power (like coal) can be transported.

Transport, the life-blood of the economic system, remains vitally important. Today much of the market for British goods is in Europe, and it is pertinent to show schoolchildren how the closer alignment of England with the mainland of Europe has led to a drift of industry to the south-east. The labour force which many of these new industries have attracted requires skills very different from those which were instrumental in developing the nineteenth-century British industrial base, a point which can be used to explain how the work which people do reflects and comments on the age in which they live. It is through these aspects of the changing lives of people that children can best be helped to appreciate the paradox of continuity and change which is history.

'That's where we used to put the casks of wine when we unloaded them from the boats which came from Spain and France', a retired docker observed, pointing to a wharf close to the school. 'Go there now and what do you find? A hotel, a ship museum and a marina.' A tired, sad comment? Nevertheless, that was the authentic voice of historical change, a voice which children need to hear.

---

* Treadmills could be mentioned in passing. We can still find evidence of their use, particularly in the kitchens of large houses where small animals were often used to turn the spit. A treadmill in working order, once used for raising water, may be seen at Carisbrooke Castle (Isle of Wight).

8   The coast

The sea has played a special part in the development of the British nation. All round the coasts we can see evidence of the struggle to master the sea, to use it for defence, trade, food and pleasure. The growth (or decline) of our ports and harbours reflect changing industrial and military needs.

Ports like Ipswich, Great Yarmouth, Lydd, Romney, and Dunwich (now no more than a small hamlet on a crumbling Suffolk cliff-face) expanded in response to an ever growing woollen industry and slowly died as steel, coal, and cotton ushered in a revolution in the economy.

Dependence on the sea has had a number of side-effects – ships had to be built and serviced and the coastline defended in time of war (evidence of this spans the Roman forts on the Saxon shore, Henry VIII's great coastal forts, nineteenth-century Martello towers, and the concrete gun emplacements of the 1940s; in addition, services were established to aid sailors – lighthouses and lightships warn against natural hazards, coastguards advise on weather and shipping move-ment, and lifeboats (and latterly helicopters) rescue and help as required. Ships and the sailors who man them offer an opportunity for work with children and it is possible to develop this study in some of the ways outlined below.

Ports

In Chapter 4, I suggest that the history of the town be studied; its growth plotted; and its development related to changes in the national economy. In this connection, we should not forget the importance of the shipbuilding yards upon which some communities came to depend. Buckler's Hard, in Hampshire, and the shipyards at Deptford and Chatham, were successful in the days of wooden ships, but were ill-suited (being some distance from the source of ore and coal) to undertake the construction of the new generation of iron ships. Children living near a port could look for evidence of ship-building (or ship repairs); it might be nothing more than a sign painted on the waterfront, a long disused dry-dock, or illustrations of the 'last launching' culled from the files of a local newspaper.

Alternatively, the town might have a number of ship-chandlers' still doing business. There may be rope/tackle/sailmakers' workshops to visit; a slipway, dry-dock, and locks to draw; and boats and oil plat-forms to photograph.

Older children could discuss the implication for a community when one industry provides the bulk of the employment. The social history of the 1920s and of the late 1970s and early 1980s provides ample evidence of the dangers.

Ports are interesting places for children to visit, but it is vital to make arrangements well in advance (a letter to the Port Super-intendent invariably results in useful literature being made available as well as relevant local addresses). Some port authorities will allow organized parties on to the quayside, while others prefer school groups to see the port from a launch. If the port is a large one, it might also prove worth while to invite a member of the police force who has responsibility for the river front to talk to the children about his work.

Lighthouses, lightships, and sea marks

These are the responsibility of the Corporation of Trinity House of Deptford Strond, London. Trinity House was founded by Henry VIII in 1514; it was a guild of shipmen and mariners, whose task was to help reduce the loss of ships along the English coastline. The guild took upon itself responsibility for 'fire beacons' and 'sea marks', the principle means of indicating the position of dangerous rocks, cliffs, and sandbanks. Lighthouses slowly replaced the fire beacons, although one lighthouse (at Dover) dates from Roman times – remin-ding us that they were known to the Ancient World. Lighthouses built on land welcome visitors during daylight hours (but not if visibility is so poor as to necessitate the sounding of fog-signals). The lightchamber is usually quite small, and since it cannot accommodate a whole class, the lighthouse is essentially a place suitable for group visits. Fully automated lighthouses cannot be visited.

A study of lighthouses may embrace both arts and sciences. They are comparatively easy to draw, and models can be wired so that the lantern lights up. Scientific terms will obviously need clarification: can we measure light? If so, how? What do we mean by 'candle-power'? How does the light beam flash? What parts do the lens and the prism play in this, and what are these? Is the fog-signal as effective as a light? Does sound travel as quickly as light?

If the light can be seen at night, its light pattern could be recorded with the aid of a stop-watch. These readings may be compared with other lighthouses and lightships in the area to show how each station has a 'call-sign' of its own.

Lifeboats and rescue services

The Lifeboat service is run by the Royal National Lifeboat Institution, which was founded by Sir William Hillary, T. Wilson and G. Hibbert in 1824 (although public interest had been aroused as early as 1785 when the first insubmersible boat had been built under the encouragement of the Prince of Wales). Lifeboats are housed all round the coast, and school groups are encouraged to visit them. The 'tour' is invariably fascinating. Apart from meeting a real sailor, the children have the opportunity to stand on deck, handle some of the equipment, and even wear life-jackets. One 9-year-old, after such an experience, remarked that he now understood a verse which had been used in assembly, 'O God, your sea is so great and my boat is so small'.

The lifeboat service works in close co-operation with the coastguards. Although coastguard stations may not be as 'romantic' as lighthouses and lifeboats, most coastguards are willing to give up their time to talk to children. As part of their work involves rescuing people who have got into difficulty often through thoughtlessness, carelessness, or bravado, try to arrange for a visit to a coastguard station whenever schoolchildren are taken to the coast. Periodically 'mock' rescues are made to test equipment and the skill of the local life-saving corps, and if this can be written into the school journey programme, if may well prove the highlight of the children's visit.

Since the Second World War an Air Sea Rescue Service (run by the RAF) has been working in close co-operation with the civil authorities. Visits to air stations are sometimes possible, but a request should be made well in advance by writing to the Commanding Officer.

Introducing the human dimension. Children can acquire detailed
information from meeting adults in their place of work. Here 9- and 10-
year-olds 'flesh out' their knowledge of the work of the RNLI from a
coxswain.

Ships

There are many maritime museums which may be visited, and a
number of historic ships which may be explored, including the *Mary
Rose* and the *Victoria* at Portsmouth, the *Cutty Sark* and *Gipsy-Moth* at
Greenwich, and the SS *Great Britain* at Bristol. Schoolchildren enjoy
comparing these historic vessels with those of modern times, e.g. the
Channel ferry, the container ship, the hovercraft, and the jet-foil.

People

Another approach to this study is to try to look for local links with
famous sailors, shipbuilders, or explorers. Statues and blue plaques
on houses provide a starting-point for initial enquiries, as do the
tombs in the local church. However, it is far better if the group can
be taken to see an exhibition connected with the person they are
studying. For examples, relics of Drake can be seen at the National
Maritime Museum; of Nelson at Portsmouth; of Henry Adams,
Nelson's shipbuilder, at Buckler's Hard, Hampshire; and of Admiral
Blake at Bridgwater, Somerset.

The sea can also be looked at through the eyes of artists (e.g.
Turner and Rowlandson), writers and poets (e.g. Masefield, Du
Maurier, and Conrad), biographers (e.g. Captains Scott and Cook),
and diarists (e.g. Samuel Pepys). 'Paintings in sound' should be used

to support the readings, and these could draw on such works as *The Hebrides* and *Calm Sea and a Prosperous Voyage* (Mendelssohn), 'Four Sea Interludes' from *Peter Grimes* (Britten), *La Mer* (Debussy), *Portsmouth Point* (Walton), *Sea Pictures* (Elgar), and Sea Symphony (Vaughan Williams). Some understanding of the customs and working life in the days of sail can be deepened by listening to (and learning) sea shanties and similar songs of labour.

Stories and legends

Stories which draw upon the sea for their inspiration are plentiful. These include legends dating from Celtic and Roman times; the real-life adventures of great explorers (Hudson, Frobisher, Drake) and villains (Christian Fletcher, Captain Kidd); sea mysteries (*Mary Celeste*); tragedies at sea (*Titanic*); novels (*Moonfleet*, *The Old Man and the Sea*, *Treasure Island*); and poetry ('The Little Revenge', 'The Rime of the Ancient Mariner').

Buildings

In some coastal towns there will be individual buildings which deserve study. Some have an interesting Custom-House or Harbour Master's Office (e.g. King's Lynn, Norfolk; Poole, Dorset; and South Quay, Great Yarmouth, Norfolk), and some inland towns may also have a link with the sea. For example, the Great Hall, Fossgate, in York, is a reminder of the time when all the foreign trade of the city was controlled by the Merchant Adventurers who built it (*c.*1357). Other subjects, for drawing, include fishermen's cottages still to be found in many coastal villages and the town houses of the prosperous eighteenth-century sea-captains. (These are often to be found in the most 'unlikely' places such as the backstreets of Deptford and Rotherhithe in south-east London.) Of course, coastal buildings also include those built for pleasure and entertainment, and many date from the mid-Victorian period. The combination of cheap railway travel and the Bank Holiday Act 1871 served to open up the coast. Tourism following on the railways meant that hotels, piers, bandstands, cliff railways, promenades, and beach shelters were built – often in the decorated ironwork and glass which was so popular with the Victorian architect.

The particular manner in which the study develops will largely be determined by the children's interest in the topic and the amount of local colour which is available. Yet of all the themes considered in this book, the sea has perhaps the widest appeal as well as providing all manner of material for display. Children's drawings, models, and descriptions can be supported by maps, notes on navigational aids (including the compass and star charts), a globe, and a timetable of local tides as well as appropriate picture and reference books. Children will want to incorporate into the display objects found along the shore – rocks and pebbles, seaweed, shells, sand samples, floats from fishing-nets, and the flotsam and jetsam of all kinds. Often the shape of these finds is enough to encourage children to create fanciful creatures of their own.

9   The countryside

Today the majority of the population of Britain live and work in towns and cities. As the drift from countryside to town has accelerated agriculture has become an even more capital-intensive industry. The effects of these changes are to be found across the landscape. Machines cut hedges and lay ditches, cultivate and drill the soil, and harvest crops. The farm labourer, skilled at hedging and ditching or cutting a straight farrow with horse and plough, is an image drawn from a past age.

The changes we may notice, as adults, are not obvious to children, for the young have grown alongside them. Moreover, town dwellers (as many of our children will be) are all too often isolated from the reality of rural life and the changing seasons. For them, and for their parents, the countryside may be little more than somewhere to spend a leisure hour or an area which has to be crossed on a journey from one town to the next. Yet as I have suggested, change is as evident in the rural setting as it is in one which is predominantly urban and industrial.

A study of the countryside can be developed in a variety of ways. Though each of the approaches listed below is distinct and individual, the links between them are sufficiently obvious that no space needs to be devoted to them here.

Farming

The enquiry 'Why do we need farms?' will probably evoke the response: 'for food.' Further questioning might lead the schoolchildren to suggest a further subdivision – i.e. the growing of plants and the keeping of animals. This somewhat simplified approach provides the starting-point for a more detailed analysis. Farms can be classified under the following headings:

Mixed
Dairy
Arable - these might grow cash-crops for sale (e.g. corn, potatoes, vegetables for freezing and canning, sugar-beet; or forage crops used to feed livestock (e.g. barley, kale, oats, grass)
Hill/livestock (sheep and cattle)
Livestock (fattening for market)
Horticulture (flowers, fruit, vegetables)
Intensive (pigs, calves, poultry kept in pens for meat and eggs)

The extent to which the above range of farm types is presented to children will obviously depend upon their age range and their experience of the countryside and the industry which it supports. The apocryphal story of the 7-year-old, who when verbally criticized by his teacher for not recognizing the picture of a sheep replied, 'It's a sheep, but I'm not sure whether it's a Cheviot or a South Down ewe', contains a warning to us all. Young children can develop a surprising degree of expertise and can quickly grasp the difference between Charolais and Devon Red cattle or Saddleback and Wessex pigs.

Many teachers use children's innate interest in animals as a peg on which to hang farm studies. Without doubt, such an approach has merit, provided that the key issue of animals as food source is not camouflaged by sentimentality.

Trips to markets and to country shows provide a worthwhile supplement to farm visits. And although the programmes and catalogues which may be obtained at these provide material which is rather too technical for children, the photographs they contain are valuable for class study books and wall displays.

A visit to a farm can be an invaluable experience to children who are growing up in an urban environment. Preparation can focus upon the type of farm being visited, and upon the geographic and climatic reasons which determine the crops which are produced. Once on site, the buildings which make up the farm complex will become an important aspect of the study.

The farm may consist of a single range of buildings – a house, a barn, and a byre – or be made up of a number of units grouped around the house and the farmyard. The design of the buildings may themselves comment upon contemporary farming and indicate

Did a Stone Age pig *really* look like this? A visit to a farm on which rare breeds are kept will help children appreciate changes in agriculture . . .

. . . particularly when related to modern 'factory' farming

something of how farming has changed over time. For example, some farm buildings in the Scottish borders serve as reminders of more lawless times. Known as 'bastles' they were fortified to give protection to people and animals.

Within the range of farm buildings several are likely to be deserving of comment. Principal among these will be the barn which, though sometimes used as a multi-purpose building, was primarily a storage place for the harvest. The size of the barn and the materials which have been employed in its construction (stone, wood, cob, brick) hint at the importance it once enjoyed.* On the contemporary farm the barn is more likely to provide cover for farm machinery than to store the seed and fodder for which it was originally designed. The design remains to offer a challenge to children. Why did the doors need to be so large? Why were they so placed? Why was ventilation so important? How was the building ventilated?

Long-established buildings, like the barn, can be compared and contrasted with their modern counterparts. Why, in times past, did farmers use cob and stone, when they now build in corrugated iron and concrete? Other buildings possibly worth notice include the dairy block, pens (for pigs and sheep), the stables (usually converted, further pointing to a decline in the importance of the horse), and the poultry unit. (Additionally, there may also be the remains of a 'wheelhouse', a reminder that the treadmill once provided the power necessary to drive farm machinery.) The silo (a tower-like building used for converting grass into silage), dovecots and pigeon lofts, and a range of beehives are other features which could provide the beginning for individual studies.

When siting a farm, the availability of an adequate water supply has always been important. Even though many modern farms can draw upon a mains water supply, evidence of a local source is often visible – i.e. pond, well, pump, or stream. Water was required for drinking both for people and animals. Less obviously, it was essential for the steam-engines which, from the Victorian period onwards, powered farm equipment. Plentiful supplies of water were also required on dairy farms and also on farms where fruit crops were processed (e.g. the cider and perry presses in Herefordshire and Somerset).

---

* A study could be made of tithe-barns. Originally these were built by religious foundations to store 'offerings' of grain made by the tenants of their estates. Many tithe-barns are still standing.

Local traditions

Since urbanization in Britain, as in other countries, is a comparatively recent development, the great majority of legends and customs are rooted in country lore. Lack of space prevents the inclusion of an extensive list, but the following areas merit consideration:

1. Folk and fairy stories, particularly where there are local links; poetry of the land.
2. Local folksongs and methods of music-making.
3. Local recipes – perhaps prepared and cooked in school.
4. Country weather-lore; country and area sayings.
5. Festivals and celebrations, e.g. well-dressing in Derbyshire; beating the bounds; plough blessing; the harvest.
6. Social dances of the area, e.g. clog, morris, horn, sword.

Local occupations and crafts

Today rural craftspeople may not be as easily found as they once were, but there remains in most communities a richness of experience that is rarely tapped by teachers. Here I am thinking of craftsmen and craftswomen like the builder of dry stone walls, the thatcher, the smith, the hedger (who invariably has a fund of knowledge about local birds and small mammals), the basket-maker, the offshore and estuary fishermen, the potter, the weaver, and the lace-maker. Each will use traditional processes and tools which have been developed over the centuries. All of these can be used to point to the part which the arts and crafts play in the enrichment of our daily lives.

Other buildings of interest

Some buildings are specific to the rural setting, others are to be found wherever people settle. When exploring a rural community, some elements such as the church, housing patterns, and the materials for building, which we have already referred to in this book, will occupy a central part of any study which is undertaken. However, the steady expansion of town and city and the destruction that this has brought in its wake have meant that the tangible links with the past are often more easily found within the rural setting such as preaching, market, and commemorative crosses; signposts and milestones; village lock-ups; almshouses and buildings erected by local benefactors; village signs; wells, pumps, and animal troughs; and pounds for straying animals.

No school visit to the countryside can ever be complete without

Learning through traditional customs – beating the parish bounds

some comment being made upon the importance of following the Country Code and its central themes:

1. Control pet dogs.
2. Keep to the footpaths.
3. Shut all gates.
4. Never leave litter.
5. Never light fires.
6. Do not pick wild flowers.

Perhaps, since the countryside is becoming even more accessible, these six strands should underpin every school trip we undertake.

10 Communication

Communication is the lifeblood of modern society. Without it, many of the things that we so readily take for granted (like the moving of goods and people and the transfer of information from one place to another) would quickly disappear. This somewhat stark approach can be the starting-point for a wide range of activities with children in the early and middle years of schooling. The question: 'why do you think that paths, trackways, and roads developed?', will trigger a range of responses. Discussion will probably lead children to comment that 'long ago' pathways were needed to link one dwelling with another and one settlement to those nearest to it. It might be suggested that pathways occurred when people and animals regularly made a particular journey – to obtain water, for example, or to reach the point where they could most easily find a river. This simple beginning might lead the more perceptive children in the group to suggest that the continual use of such 'ways' reduced vegetation along them, allowing travellers on horse or with wagon to move reasonably freely between one settlement and another. Conjecture and reflection of this kind can provide valuable insights into the level of children's historical understanding and indicate to the perceptive teacher how effective is the programme which the group are being invited to follow.

Road transport has for long been a favourite theme in primary schools – embracing as it does over 6,000 years of history. Invariably it is treated developmentally. A lesson on the Celtic trackways is followed in rapid succession by others on Roman roads, the medieval wagon ways, the Elizabethan post-roads, and the turnpikes, culminating in a film strip showing the construction of the latest motorway. Before I criticize this well-tried approach, I must commend it for its simplicity: it does allow a blanket coverage of almost everything from travelling by foot to the development of the wheel and the internal-combustion engine. Furthermore, the road can be shown as an instrument of military power and as an essential part in the economic life of the community. We can compare the methods employed by Vespasian, Telford, McAdam, and their latter-day counterparts.

For all its neatness, such an approach has inherent weaknesses. Every change in human affairs is the consequence of a whole range of subtle, sometimes hidden, influences. Technological changes almost invariably come about as a direct result of need. We would not need to ravish the countryside with six-lane motorways were it not for the development of the internal-combustion engine. Even had the petrol-engine been invented, the family car could only become a reality because mass-production techniques, born of the Industrial Revolution, could be applied to vehicle production. The use of the internal-combustion engine for individual and family travel is dependent upon ever more sophisticated methods of oil exploration and processing (and therefore upon the scientific discoveries which make this possible).

The danger of approaching a historical study by using one element (e.g. roads) to leap from past to present is that the technological, human, and social dimensions are largely ignored. The Romans might well have needed military roads – to construct them, this 'need' placed demands upon the map-makers, the engineers, the craftsmen who made the equipment that would be used by the artisans, and the labourers who cleared forests, and carried and laid the stones. Initially the military need may have been of paramount importance, but in periods of peace civilian needs determined the repair of the roads and their further development.

The horizontal theme *can* be a peg upon which to hang a project. If it is used, it must be most carefully constructed. Children need to be helped to grasp the paradox of continuity within change which is central to an understanding of history, particularly when the changes being discussed were shaped by elements outside the immediate area of study.

With schoolchildren a number of varying approaches can be attempted in a study of roads. The most straightforward approach seeks to answer questions focusing on the roads nearest to where the children live. Thus we can begin by asking: 'where does it go to?' The immediate answer of the two nearest villages or towns can thus be used as the point of departure for map-work and this, in turn, leads to a detailed study of the Ordnance Survey map for the area: has the road a Ministry of Transport classification? Has it a number? What does the number mean?

This study may develop in any number of ways. If it is designed to relate road transport to modern industry, the nearest large road to the school can be used for a traffic count. Remember to take the count over the same period each day, say, for one week, to obtain some base figures from which to work. For example, a count could be taken over five school-days of both north- and south-bound traffic between 9.45 and 10.00 a.m. and 3.15 and 3.30 p.m. Fifteen-minute counts taken at other times during the day can then be related to these figures. Counts can be broken down into the kinds of traffic using the road (lorry, bus, car, taxi, motor-cycle). The statistics so gained can then be pictorially represented (in graphs and pie-charts) – an area in which art, environmental studies, and mathematics fuse admirably.

Another practical study centres upon 'street furniture'. What can be found along the roadside which points to its present function or to changing use over time? Most roadways and streets are a mixture of past and present. Modern roadsigns, traffic-lights, and parking-meters have not completely replaced finger-posts and milestones. Garages and motels may have deposed the stable and the coaching inn, but hints of the horse still remain in roadside water troughs, inn signs, mounting-blocks, and in the iron boot cleaner outside many a street-door. Horses were much dirtier to run than cars! Other elements which could be studied include street names: how many different forms – road, way, gardens, row, park, heights, lane, path, wynd – are to be found within a half-mile radius of school, and do the names selected have any particular significance? Additionally, the position and type of road signs, street-lights, telephone kiosks, and post-boxes may be noted. Obviously studies of this kind should involve the use of maps, past and present, which enables the concept of land utilization to be introduced and comparisons made between the use of land during different historical periods.

In studying roads it will be difficult to avoid those elements particular to them – e.g. toll-houses, toll-gates, and toll-bridges – and in low-lying areas the road might be lined with ditches and dykes (as in The Fens), or it may have to cross a river by a bridge or a ford. This brings us to ask the sorts of question which occur again and again throughout this book: how old is this construction? What materials have been used to build it? – e.g. wood, stone, brick, metal, reinforced concrete? Why are stone and brick preferred to wood? Do we know who built it and for what purpose, e.g. for foot passengers, wagons, cars, or trains? Are there any interesting stories about it?

Bridges can be taken as the starting-point for a wide range of historical and scientific studies. Apart from providing much to draw and model, children can be encouraged to note certain things about each bridge they see: what is the shape of the cutwaters on the upstream and downstream faces of the pillars? What shape have the arches? Is the bridge decorated in any way? Is there evidence that there was once a ford or a ferry at this site? (The direction in which the road runs often provides some indication.) How many different kinds of bridge can be found near school – e.g. beam, arch (or tied arch), cantilever (or cantenary) suspension, swing bridge, drawbridge (or bridge with two rising bascules, as Tower Bridge, London)?

A study of roads can also provide an entry point into literature and legends; indeed they occupy a prominent part in the literature of childhood. Therefore, a project on roads could be linked to language work; it was on a road that Jack swopped his mother's cow for magic beans; that Whittington heard the church bells; that the three little pigs met the men with straw and sticks and bricks; and that an unfortunate old lady lost her petticoats! But before we dismiss these examples as the whimsy of childhood, think too of other writers who have been affected by the 'mystery of the road': Laurie Lee writes of 'the traditional forces which sent many generations along this road'; John Masefield of 'treading the rocky road of no return to some immortal end'; Robert Frost of the 'two roads which diverged in a yellow wood'; Christina Rossetti of the road which 'winds uphill all the way'; and Rudyard Kipling of the ghostly men and women who still ride along the road 'closed seventy years ago'.

The introduction to a historical study through literature is valid. It helps bring the past to life, encouraging children to imagine 'what might have been'. This can be deepened further by presenting the road in the form of a time chart.

Let us assume that the road which passes the school joins the London–Dover road. Who might have travelled along it? It was certainly part of Watling Street, and so would have known the tread of legionaries marching between Rome and Londinium. Although it is conjecture that St Augustine rode along this road to Canterbury, Norman soldiers must have used it regularly *en route* for Rochester and its castle. The murder of Thomas à Becket brought a new group of travellers – pilgrims (of whom Chaucer was one) travelling from London and Dover to pray at his shrine in Canterbury. The dissolution of the monasteries under Henry VIII did not halt the flow of travellers, including merchants and bankers *en route* for the Low Countries; soldiers embarking for continental wars; Cavaliers fleeing from Cromwell; Huguenots fleeing from France; Samuel Pepys visiting His Majesty's dockyards at Chatham; French nobles escaping from the Terror; Charles Dickens visiting his house in Kent; and

British troops evacuating Dunkirk. Of course, this method of approach is appropriate to almost any important road we care to choose, and if the school is situated close to one of the truly ancient trackways (like Pedder's Way, in Norfolk), the study is all the richer.

In addition to writing descriptive and imaginative pieces about the road and the people who used it (supplemented with extracts from contemporary documents, diaries, and novels), a large wall frieze might also be made. Join sheets of sugar paper longways to make a frieze, 35 cm deep by 350 cm long, and paint this in a pastel shade. This will form the road. Divide the class into small groups and invite each to draw a group of travellers to represent a different period in history – from pre-Roman times to the present day. These groups are worked on sugar paper, 30 cm deep by 50 cm long, in crayon, oil pastel, paint, or fabric scraps. These 'travellers' are then cut out and mounted on to the paper frieze. The aim should be to make the travellers typical of their time – did they walk, ride, travel by litter, sedan chair, chariot, stage-coach, mail coach, steam-car, penny farthing, a 'horseless carriage', a motor-coach or a tram car? What did they wear? How long did it take to make a journey between two neighbouring towns?

The frieze could be supported by a picture map of the road, marrying together all its features from across the centuries. If this were attempted for the Great North Road, the Great West Road, Ermine Street, the Fosse-way, or the road from Holyhead to Shrewsbury, it would surely provide the average class of 10-year-olds with enough material for at least a year of environmental studies.

In the eighteenth century the development of new technology enabled a network of canals to be developed. Although the construction of canals between 1760 and 1850 was as dramatic as that of the railways, the subsequent development of canals tends to feature very rarely in primary school studies. This is a pity, for canals and waterways contain much to interest children – from wild life to lock machinery. The bridges, in particular, deserve study. As well as conventional foot and road bridges (usually beautifully proportioned stone structures), swing bridges are quite common near docks and harbours; 'drawbridges' may also be found on some lengths of canal (e.g. the Oxford Canal). On these bridges a section is raised for canal traffic by means of a counterbalance. In addition to sketching and model-making, canal bridges are worth examining closely for visual historical 'clues': is there a commemorative plaque on the bridge to indicate when it was built or the name of the architect? If the bridge is built of stone or brick, is there a protective band on the corner of the soffit on the towpath side to prevent the tow-rope from wearing away the stone facing? If the bridge is of iron, is the name of the manufacturer still visible, or the name of the works in which the metal was smelted? Aqueducts are less common than bridges, but many are still in existence. Pontcysyllte, for example, which now carries pleasure craft to Llangollen (121 feet above the River Dee) was once part of the Ellesmere Canal. Some aqueducts were made of stone, others of metal.

In any event, a study of the route of the canal or an Ordnance Survey map will indicate something of the physical problems which the canal-builders had to overcome. Aqueducts were one method of controlling water levels, another was of course the lock.

Working locks are to be found on rivers and canals and the principle is sufficiently simple for even young children to grasp. Sometimes locks were built in 'flights' – usually where it was necessary to raise the canal up the side of a valley. One of the most famous flights is on the Kennet and Avon Canal near Devizes, in Wiltshire, which consists of 29 'steps'.

So much for the bank, what of the traffic which the canal carries? If the canal is still in use, maps and diagrams could be made to show barge routes and the time which it takes to travel by water between neighbouring towns, so that comparisons may be made in road/rail communications. Canal barges are not difficult to model. The child who enjoys work with a fine brush will certainly enjoy decorating the boat's superstructure.

By the towpath toll-houses and pump-houses might also be discovered, though many nowadays are in such a sad state of repair as to be almost unrecognizable. Pump-houses were required because the canal-builders needed to ensure that an adequate reserve of water was always readily available. When a canal crossed a hillside, water sometimes had to be pumped from below if no natural high-level source was available.

Tolls for the use of the canal were charged on mileage. Iron mileposts can still be found on many towpaths. Indeed we are fortunate that iron was the material of the canal age, for all manner of interesting inscriptions and signposts remain and many well worth recording with rubbings.

If the children have made a study of inns near school, they would find it worth while to make note of canal-side inns and their signboards. These often reflect the canal age, rejoicing in such titles as 'The Jolly Bargeman', 'The Towpath', 'The Barge', and 'The Navigation'. In the heyday of the canals these inns would also have had stables for the boatmen's horses, and the observant child might well be able to discover where these were situated.

Canal development (like that of the railways a century later) had a considerable influence on the growth of towns. Thus in the forty

years between 1801 and 1841 the population of Birmingham increased
by 112,000, that of Leeds by 99,000, and that of Manchester by
180,000. Even towns which could hardly be considered pacemakers
on the industrial front showed considerable population increases over
the same period – the population of Cambridge increased by 14,000,
Bath by 20,000, York by 12,000, Reading by 9,000, and Oxford by
14,000. Apart from Birmingham, whose first navigable waterway
dates from 1772, all of the towns mentioned had had some form of
inland navigation since 1760.

Older children – especially if they have been fortunate enough to
have experienced a school tour on a canal barge – would benefit from
visiting the Inland Waterways Museum at Stoke Bruerne, Northamptonshire, which contains everything from decorated barges, water-
cans, pumps, and pictures to momentoes of the gangs who did the
digging.

The advent of the moving steam-locomotive was marked by a
decline in the construction and use of canals. For the many children
who do not live near a canal, the railway usually provides the oldest
evidence of our development as an industrial nation.

Railways, the growth of which mushroomed after the successful
completion of the Liverpool and Manchester line (1826–30) by George
and Robert Stephenson, are still with us. The tracks follow the lines
laid down by the early pioneers, and their bridges, viaducts, and
cuttings are a continual reminder of the skill of the Victorian
engineer. Even in this age of railway closure the evidence remains.

Thus, while it is important that children should be aware how
railways developed piecemeal, with numerous small companies
establishing local lines, our starting-point can be more immediate.
Look at the Ordnance Survey map of the locality: where does the
railway run? Is its path straight, does it cling to a ridge, or bend
gently to take advantage of a river valley? Did the geology of the area
need to be taken into account? What evidence is there of the work of
the 'navvies' who cut viaducts and built embankments, so that tracks
ran on a level 'bed'? The files of local newspapers might throw some
light on apparently odd twists and turns that cannot otherwise be
understood. The construction of railways was not always popular
with landowners, who were not always prepared to accept compensa-
tion for the soot, smoke, and dirt of the early engines.

Following the railway track on a map might naturally lead to following it on foot. On this walk (particularly in a country area) the
children should look for evidence of the early pioneers. These are
often to be found on the ironwork of bridges and on the metal notices
which abound on any length of track (particularly near stations, level-
crossings, and signal-boxes). Many of these signs were erected before

The age-of-steam recaptured in the headstone in Bromsgrove Churchyard to Thomas Scaife, who was killed in a railway accident on the Birmingham and Gloucester Railway in November 1884

the passing of the Railway Act 1921. This Act created the London, Midland and Scottish Railway (LMS); the London North-Eastern Railway (LNER); the Great Western Railway (GWR); and the Southern Railway (SR), by amalgamating 120 small companies. Thus in addition to notices placed by the LMS, LNER, GWR, and SR, many signs still bear the names or initials of their original operators – e.g. the London and South-Western, the London and North-Western, the London, Chatham and Dover, the Southampton and Dorchester, the Lancaster and Preston, the Newcastle and North Shields, and the Greenwich and Blackwall railways. Where the notices are not too near the track – i.e. on stations, by pedestrian crossings, or in country lanes – rubbings could be taken with crayon on detail paper. The walk should take in the local station, but in order to visit permission must first be obtained from the Divisional Manager of the region (the station-master will have his address).

Railways of course had a tremendous effect upon Britain and whole new areas were opened up; towns appeared where none had existed before. Swindon, Eastleigh, and Crewe owe as much to the Cheap Trains Act 1844 as more romantic places owe to long dead City Fathers. Barrow-in-Furness (Cumbria) had 250 people before the railway came in 1841, while in 1881 over 47,000 were living there.

Local studies might suggest answers to such questions as: where does the railway line go to? What important towns are on its route? How long ago was the line established? If the town once had a railway and the line is now closed, what railway buildings remain? For what are they now used?

Model-making based on a railway theme allows for a variety of work from detailed engines assembled from commercially produced kits to less accurate (though more educationally valid) models made from junk and card. Railway architecture is another possible development – models being made on a scale which would allow for their incorporation in toy track layouts.

The study may be extended through visits to the Transport Museum, Covent Garden, London; the Science Museum (which boasts the original *Rocket*); and those at Swindon and York. It is well to remember that non-specialist museums often have transport sections. For example, William Hedley's *Wylam Dilly* (1814) may be seen at the Royal Scottish Museum, Edinburgh.

Railway preservation societies often encourage party bookings and, in any event, a ride on a steam train is something of an event. Finally, one can try taking the sounds of the railway into the classroom. Argo have a long list of sound portraits in steam, though for me Honegger's tone poem, *Pacific 321*, evokes the living power of a great locomotive rather better than the rattle of the real thing!

Railways continue to play an important part in our communication network. In recent years their principal competitor, road transport, has been joined by another – air travel.

Air transport and the changes which the coming of an airport can make to a community merit some mention here. Its inclusion in a class study will largely depend upon the proximity of the school to a civilian airport and could centre upon the impact it makes upon the area: what specific services does a large airport need – e.g. road and rail links, housing for its labourforce, and specialist facilities (catering, aircraft servicing, hotels)? This can lead to an enquiry into why a particular site was selected: what sort of landscape is most suitable? How does the airport relate to population centres in Britain? How much land does one runway (suitable for a jumbo jet) consume? What advantages are brought to a local community when a nearby airport expands? Are there disadvantages? Should concern for the habitat be allowed to override perceived economic needs?

A study of communication – by land, water, or air – serves to indicate how developments in technology lead to fundamental changes in life-style. Just as the railway opened up the coast to countless day trippers in the 1880s and 1890s, the development of the jet engine has brought new possibilities of travel. Within three generations a revolution has occurred. Comparatively few children who were at school in the 1920s and 1930s could boast of journeys made and places seen. Today it is commonplace for children to travel in Britain and abroad. Undoubtedly, such experience plays an invaluable part in their development.

John Stow, in his *Survey of London*, observed that 'The world runs on wheels with many whose parents were glad to go on foot'. Times have changed but little, but now the wheels go faster and cover greater distances. What we as parents and teachers need to ensure is that speed of travel is never allowed to become more important than the reason for travelling. Young children, like adults, must be given the opportunity to stand and stare.

11 Museums and stately homes

In Britain one is never far from a museum or a stately home, and that this is as true for a child living in a country village as for one living in London or Glasgow, means that collections can play a very real part in young people's learning. Whether we take a school party to a national institution like the British Museum or to see a small 'personal' exhibition in a Tudor long gallery, the same general principles apply. These may be briefly summarized as follows.

1. *What are we going to see?* It seems to me essential that children on school visits are made aware beforehand of the sort of things they might be expected to find. This will involve preparation on the teacher's part, for children are unlikely to get much from visiting the excellent Roman collections at Cirencester or St Albans, for example, if their current work has embraced the Thames Basin to the exclusion of all else! The more specialist is the collection, the greater will be the need for adequate preparation. The way in which we present the collection in this pre-visit discussion will of course vary with the interests, abilities, and age of the schoolchildren concerned. For 6-year-olds going to the Science Museum, London, for the first time, it might entail little more than looking at pictures of aircraft, and 7-year-olds visiting Hardwick Hall could hardly do better than watch a film strip illustrating social life in the late sixteenth century; and less able 10-year-olds might better understand the Maiden Castle exhibits, at Dorchester, through a story which illustrates quite incidentally the campaign of the Emperor Vespasian.

2. *How are we going to work?* Here the very nature of children's

learning bridges age barriers: children learn by looking and talking and handling – and it is a sad reflection on many learning situations that this last essential ingredient is lacking, even in those museums which otherwise operate an utterly praiseworthy schools service.

If they are to make sketches and take notes, the children will need to be given a clipboard; duplicate pencils are also essential. (In every class there is at least one child who loses a pencil *en route*.) Fibre-tipped pens and ball-points have a definite advantage over most other writing equipment in most respects – they do not require sharpening, clip securely into pockets, and are excellent for sketchwork. If large drawings are to be attempted, these are best worked in wax crayon or oil pastel on sugar paper. Portable tape recorders make possible accurate on-the-spot verbal descriptions of interesting exhibits and also save much time if lengthy captions are to be used as source material for follow-up work on return to school. Cameras may also be taken into many of the smaller museums, but permission should be obtained before they are used.

Again, it is difficult to be specific on the best way for children to work outside the classroom. Personally, I do not give children quiz-sheets or worksheets; in my experience these tend to encourage a superficial approach and I am certain that a child who has drawn accurately a Chippendale chair will have learned far more about the Georgians than he/she would have done by completing a question-naire with appropriate one-word answers. Meaningful learning is in fact more likely to take place if individuals are encouraged to look at things which interest them (the quick method tells children what to look for and, by implication, what to ignore).

If the group are allowed to touch exhibits, writing can stem from the experience; indeed some museums even have handling trays, so that this approach is actively encouraged.

Children are interested in people's lives. A fruitful approach is to link the visit, whenever appropriate, to the life of a person who once lived in the house or made the collection. This identification with a real person might result in the preparation of a simple biography, encouraging children to contextualize their learning, fitting a particular life within the broader framework of the times. This would mean, then, that contemporary attitudes to art, architecture, politics, and science and technology, as well as such things as religious beliefs, leisure activities, manners, and fashion, could all be touched upon. In this connection, writers, musicians, and artists have much to offer since selection of their work (written extracts, recordings, reproductions) can be used in school to further deepen an apprecia-tion of their life and times.

Not all stately homes (or museums housed in them) will have

SURVEY SHEET

AREA VISITED   London

BUILDING/PLACE Chiswick House

Date   May 9th 1988

<u>Things of interest, my drawings and notes</u>

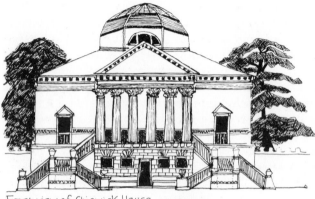

Front view of Chiswick House

Plan

Garden view of Chiswick House

The Gallery at Chiswick House

Richard Boyle the third <u>Earl of Burlington</u> was the Architect who designed this house at Chiswick. When he was young he travelled abroad a lot especially in Italy. He was particularly influenced by the work of <u>Andrea Palladio</u> (1508-80) Burlington was born in 1694 and he died in 1753. In about 1714 when he was in Rome he met <u>William Kent</u> (1685-1748). Kent came from a very different background but he and Burlington became good friends and worked closely together for most of their lives.

Chiswick House was built in about 1723 to 1729. It is a "model house" mainly of staterooms and it was attached to the earlier family home. It is closely modelled on the Villa Rotunda in Vicenza by Palladio. The ground floor is of Portland stone. Originally this floor was Burlington's library. The upper floors are stucco. William Kent designed the interiors which were based on the ideas of <u>Inigo Jones</u> (1573-1652). The gardens were landscaped by Kent who tried to develop a "natural" look. There are rows of statues, including one of Palladio and one of Jones.

Figure 13 **Survey of a stately home**

clearly identifiable links with a particular person. Another approach is to invite the group to look closely at any portraits of children which may be on display. A range of questions may then suggest themselves: what kind of person do you think this portrait conveys? What do the clothes (and the other elements within the portrait) tell you about him or her? How are they standing (or sitting or moving)? Can one 'capture' this posture? Having talked about a portrait in this way, each child should be encouraged to choose a portrait and to prepare a written description of the 'message' which it gives.

If a contextual approach is attempted, make sure that attention is given to a broader spectrum of society than those reflected through expensive furniture, extensive houses, and extravagant portraiture. The comfortable life of the squire and his family was built upon the unremitting toil of a far greater number of men and women who laboured 'below stairs'. It is comparatively easy to help children appreciate some aspects of a servant's life, by enumerating the fireplaces to be cleared and relit each day and the amount of wood and coal to be carried to each, by drawing attention to the difficulties of cleaning pots and pans without recourse to modern detergents, and of housework without electrical appliances – and the bleakness of a parlourmaid's bedroom.

This approach can often be supported with archival material. For example, account books are often available which show domestic and estate expenditure. Through them it is possible to discover the number of servants employed and something of the tasks which they performed. It may be possible to obtain photocopies of maps and plans of the house and estate during different stages of its development. Any collection could be 'brought up to date' with an illustrated guide and plan prepared by the children following on a school visit. 3. *How long should the party stay?* Little is achieved if children view museums and stately homes as places in which they march round crocodile-fashion, slowly becoming more and more tired, gazing at case upon case of irrelevant exhibits. It is important that each visit should fire the child's imagination, deepen his or her understanding and provide the stimulus for further work in school. Over-stimulation is short-sighted. It is possible to see so much that one ends up by remembering nothing.

It may appear that the preceding paragraphs assume that the teacher has had opportunity to visit the collection in advance. If the visit is being made as part of a school journey programme, this may not have been possible. It is in such cases that the curator (or schools' officer) can be of tremendous use; the type of help forthcoming will obviously depend upon the facilities which the site has at its disposal.

'Living Museums' often contain 'living exhibits', like these 10-year-olds taking a lesson in an Elizabethan schoolroom

There might be a children's lecture-room, complete with a range of visual aids (as at Newport, Gwent) or a studio (as at the Geffrye Museum, London), or the curator might have information on local sites worth visiting (as at Dumfries) or be in touch with local experts in their own field who are prepared to talk to school parties. At the least, a catalogue can be obtained which will indicate relevant subject areas and hours of admission. The services which a museum provides are rarely advertised, and pre-visit contact between teacher and curator is surely a necessity.

The past twenty years have seen many developments in the display techniques employed by museums. Open museums in which children quite literally can walk into a bygone age are of particular interest. For example, at York it is possible to stroll down a nineteenth-century street, gaze at shop fronts and wander into the forecourt of an inn to examine a stage-coach. At St Fagans (Cardiff) there are furnished cottages illustrating the slowly changing social and economic conditions in the principality since the Middle Ages. Similarly, to visit Beamish or Coalbrookdale is to experience something of industrial England.

Visits to collections (be they within old houses or modern museums) can be given a sharper focus by choosing particular elements for study. For example, children could be invited to draw and make notes about artefacts which reflect the way in which materials have been used. Thus each child builds up a personal collection of drawings in which the chosen artefacts reflect use of wood, metal, glass, bone, clay, cloth, leather, ivory, horn (and even plastic). On return to school, these drawings and supporting notes can be classified: why was metal chosen for one range of artefacts? Why was clay much more suitable than wood for others?

This approach focusing upon specifically prescribed aspects of a collection can be applied in other ways. For example, children could be asked to make their own 'collection' of furniture (one table, one stool, one bed, one chair), of hand-tools used for cutting (one used in gardening, one in craft, one in the kitchen), of types of fastening (clothes, doors, boxes, windows), or of mechanical toys. In similar vein, children may be invited to become detectives, looking for evidence which points to the ways in which food was prepared, cooked and eaten during a particular historical period or of evidence which suggests that methods of heating and lighting have changed since a building was first erected.

Concentration by each child upon his or her own way of looking, leading to individual discoveries, will enable an eventual classroom display to feature a wide range of contrasting yet complementary elements. It will also achieve much more than this. By working in this way, we encourage each child to look and to observe and thereby to discover something of the joy of having a personal (as opposed to an imposed) interest. As adults, if our role is to help children to gain some insight into their culture, their curiosity about the past needs actively to be fostered. This can only happen when each child develops a seeing eye and an enquiring mind, skills perhaps almost impossible to develop through worksheets and prescribed exercises.

12 Extending the experience

The focus of this book has been on how exploration of the man-made environment can be used to develop children's appreciation of the past. By taking children into the world outside the classroom to study buildings and the artefacts associated with them, the teacher acknowledges the central place which the senses play in the development of understanding. Looking down from a castle keep, smelling a dungeon's mustiness, experiencing that evocative silence in a Saxon church, or touching a stone carving made by a Roman mason, are examples of how the senses can deepen our historical imagination and fantasy. Unlike facts (which are easily forgotten), the questions which come from looking, seeing, and experiencing tend to evoke personal enquiry: the skills of research which can be fostered as a consequence of personal (rather than directed) questioning last throughout a lifetime.

Although the great majority of the suggestions contained in this book involve the active participation of the young learner, one essential element has so far been ignored. Exploring an old lighthouse or wandering across a battlefield like, say, Culloden Moor may provide invaluable experience, yet the child may remain a detached outsider, an intruder from another age. An important element of the teacher's task is therefore to attempt to merge present into past by constructing situations through which children can have their perceptions heightened and their understandings deepened.

A well-established and effective approach is through 'Theatre in Education' (TIE), which uses an approach based upon historical reconstruction. Through it children explore a precisely defined period

Learning through re-enactment. The National Trust Young Theatre at Bodiam, in Sussex, re-live some of the tensions of the Civil War (10–12-year-olds) . . .

. . . and at Osterley Park re-create life on the Home Front, 1917 (12- and 13-year-olds)

of the past, its customs, language, and the arts, relating these to specific events and happenings which shaped the belief and attitudes of the people who were alive at that time.

Theatre in Education is built on the belief that schoolchildren will develop in the process of historical reconstruction a degree of contextual understanding, the ability to set people within their time, and to use their deepening historical imagination to fantasize and empathize with people who lived during the period being studied. It may take many forms. At its simplest level, it occurs when a group of children reconstruct a period of the past within their own class or school; for example, a group of children studying the Victorian period might follow a typical school-day of the 1880s. To achieve this, the classroom furniture needs to be rearranged and the walls, containing only a picture of the Queen and a map of the world, made rather drab and forbidding. The teacher, appropriately dressed and equipped with a blackboard and easel, cane, punishment-book, and a large free-standing abacus, offers his/her charges a diet of sums and copperplate writing worked with chalk on slates. The class will follow a timetable which begins with a Bible reading and prayers and consists of mental and written arithmetic, spelling, the chanting of tables (2 to 12), grammatical exercises, class readings from Charles Kingsley's *Water Babies*, and the recitation of Tennyson (from memory). Playtime toys would be restricted to skipping-ropes, spinning-tops, and hoops (hopscotch is permissible). Midday lunch would also echo stable Victorian foods – hot potato, hunks of bread and cheese. Children and the teaching staff with whom they are working will be dressed throughout the day in period costume (prepared in advance as part of the background studies for the 'day').

Obviously the elements which can be fitted into such an event are limitless. For example, the class might be visited by the local 'rector' enquiring the reason for absences from Sunday School, or the headteacher might introduce the 'School Board Inspector' to the class and then depart, leaving the Inspector to administer the test appropriate to the 'standard' (or year) of the children. In one school in which I worked this idea was extended to the whole of the junior school, and re-enactments in which the whole-school community (children, parents, teachers, and ancillary staff) took part featured a Medieval Christmas, the Home Front in the Second World War, and an Edwardian Music-hall.

If a re-enactment is to be attempted, care must be taken to choose a theme which is comprehensible to the schoolchildren. Re-enactments are *not* theatre in the sense that lines are learned and actions memorized; however, they are drama in which children re-act one to another, in a fashion and style appropriate to the period which is being explored.

The study of a local fair led to model-making . . .

. . . and its re-creation within the school (5–11-year-olds – and their parents!)

At a more sophisticated level, TIE is offered to schools through local education authorities, museum education officers, the owners of historical buildings, and through agencies such as the National Trust (NT); TIE, which employs actors to 'lead' children into an exploration of a study of the past, has been pioneered by the National Trust Education Unit. The period offered to participating schools for the season (spring to autumn) is first carefully researched. The chosen period – e.g. Queen Elizabeth I, the Civil War, the First World War: the Home Front, and the Armada year – is selected because it provides sufficient opportunity for extemporization and is relevant to children's studies and bears some relationship to NT properties across the country. The director of the Young National Trust theatre provides participating schools with contextual information about the period being studied to ensure that children are well prepared for the experience.

The children who take part in these re-enactments on NT properties (some 90 children for each three-hour presentation) are encouraged to become more deeply involved in the 'happening': the task of the actors is to respond sensitively to the children's ideas and to set them within the framework of the story-line which has been prepared.

Re-enactments (fancifully called 'Living History') are undoubtedly an effective means of teaching, provided that the participants are given roles which allow them to have some power and influence. One historical re-enactment devised by a county museum's service was roundly criticized by visiting educationists because the children taking part were given menial roles. The adults swaggered in rich Edwardian costume, the children (parlourmaids, chambermaids, bootblacks, gardeners, and pot-boys) watched in quiet submission. The response, from one 11-year-old, that she had learned something: 'the boredom and leg ache of a parlourmaid', did throw some light on Edwardian life. Sadly the experience could have been much more positive!

Learning by living through an enactment should allow the children to experience within a contextual setting something of the reality of life in times past. Cleaning a greasy pot, in which schoolchildren have cooked their midday meal on a log-burning range, will go some way towards helping the children to appreciate just how food was prepared and cooked (as well as how it tasted); the quantity of wood required to keep the fire alight (as well as the labour involved in fetching it); and the difficulty of cleaning pots and pans using hot water and earth or sand.

Undoubtedly, this approach to children's learning will develop even more extensively in the future. Many institutions (e.g. the Royal Opera House, Covent Garden) have come to realize that by offering schools the opportunity to draw upon their particular expertise, in making knowledgeable adults available to explore ideas with school-children, the gulf which separates the real world from that of the classroom can be bridged.

The world beyond the classroom is one in which the children and their parents live, move, work, and play. Our task as teachers, then, is also to draw upon this richness which exists on the other side of the playground wall.

Children's understanding of their heritage will not develop by sitting within a classroom, the silent recipients of a torrent of words. Such appreciation grows from regular exposure, and it is our task to make sure that this occurs. The cynic might be prompted to enquire why we should bother: is it not far easier to regard knowledge as something which is mediated through the teacher? Is the learner's emotional and spiritual response *so* important?

To which observation there can be but one response: today's children are the conservationists or the vandals of tomorrow. At the least, let us try to give today's children some insight into those things (buildings and landscapes) which deserve to be preserved. It is towards the development of such perceptions that this book has been directed, for our heritage lives ultimately not in buildings or in artefacts, but in our human responses to them. By exposing children to the richness of the past, in all its diverse forms, these responses are most likely to be realized.

Appendix 1: Source material

Photocopies of source material which will prove of great use in developing the environmental studies programme for a school can often be obtained through the local authority's museums and library service. The following categories of material are worth consulting:

Audio-visual records	films or video tapes of events which feature the area being studied; audio tapes of stories and events told in local dialect, folk songs, folk music.
Council and committee papers	burial records; electoral registers; minutes; ratebooks.
Cuttings	local and national newspapers.
Directories	commercial directories, e.g. Kelly, Kemp, Pigot, Robson, and Smith.
Illustrations	drawings, photographs, postcards, prints, and transparencies.
Legal records	Census returns; national records; school log-books.
Local societies	Minutes; magazines; reports of local historical society.

Maps	local surveys; street maps; village and town plans; Ordnance Survey maps.
Newspapers and periodicals	local and national; parish and local society magazines.
Parochial and religious records	parish registers; ratebooks; Nonconformist and chapel records; Poor Law Overseers' records.
Records (various)	civil defence papers, 1939–45; private business records; deeds, family, and estate records
Special collections	material donated by local families, industries, etc.

Appendix 2:
A bibliography

Architecture and landscape

Braun, H. (1951) *Introduction to English Medieval Architecture*, London: Faber.
Hoskins, W.G. (1979) *Reading the Landscape*, London: BBC Publications.
Muir, Richard (1981) *Reading the Landscape*, London: Michael Joseph.

Customs

Hartley, D. (1979) *The Land of England*, London: Macdonald.

Defence

Brown, Allen, R. (1976 edn) *English Castles*, London: Batsford.
Johnston, Forde (1979) *Great Medieval Castles of Britain*, London: Guild
    Publishing. (BCA).
Simpson, Douglas (1969) *Castles in England and Wales*, London: Batsford.

Ecclesiastical

Anderson, M.D. (1971) *History and Imagery in English Churches*, London: John
    Murray.
Braun, H. (1970) *Parish Churches*, London: Faber.
Braun, H. (1971) *English Abbeys*, London: Faber.
Hogg, Gary (1972) *Priories and Abbeys of England*, Newton Abbot: David &
    Charles.
Jones, Lawrence (1978) *The Beauty of English Churches*, London: Constable.
Smith, E. *et al.* (1976) *English Parish Churches*, London: Thames & Hudson.
Watkins, P. and Hughes, E. (1980) *Here's the Church*, London: Julia MacRae.

Industrial

Bailey, B. (1982) *Industrial Heritage of Britain*, London: Ebury Press.
Briggs, A. (1979) *Iron Bridge to Crystal Palace*, London: Thames & Hudson.
Freeman, Allen (1979) *Railways in Britain*, London: Marshall Cavendish.
Hadfield, C. (1968) *The Canal Age*, Newton Abbot: David & Charles.
Hudson, K. (1976) *Archeology of Industry*, London: Bodley Head.
de Marc, Eric (1975 edn) *Bridges of Britain*, London: Batsford.

Local history

Anderson, M.D. (1967) *History by the Highway*, London: Faber.
Cameron, K. (1982 edn) *English Place Names*, London: Batsford.
Ekwall, E. (1960) *Concise Oxford Dictionary of English Place Names*, Oxford: Oxford University Press.
Hoskins, W.G. (1967) *Fieldwork in Local History*, London: Faber.
Hoskins, W.G. (1984 edn) *Local History in England*, London: Longman.
Iredale, D. (1974) *Local History Research*, Chichester: Phillimore.
Pluckrose, H. (1984) *Look Around – Outside*, London: Heinemann.
Prosser, P. (1982) *The World on Your Doorstep*, London: McGraw-Hill.
Rider, P. (1983) *Local History – a Handbook*, London: Batsford.
Stephens, W.B. (1973) *Sources for Local History*, Manchester: Manchester University Press.
English place names: see English Place Names Society editions, published by Cambridge University Press.

Photography

Buchannan, A. (1983) *Photographing Historic Buildings*, London: HMSO.

Vernacular architecture

Brunskill, R. (1971) *Vernacular Architecture*, London: Faber.
Cook, O. (1982) *English Cottages and Farmhouses*, London. Thames & Hudson.
Muir, R. (1982) *Lost Villages of Britain*, London: Michael Joseph.
Peel, J.H.B. (1972) *An Englishman's Home*, London: Cassell.
Taylor, C. (1983) *Village and Farmstead*, London: George Philip.
West, T. (1971) *The Timberframe House*, Newton Abbot: David & Charles.

General reference

Falkins, M. and Gillingham, J. (1979) *Historical Atlas of Britain*, London: Granada Publishing.
Freeman-Grenville, G. (1979) *Atlas of British History*, London: Rex Collings.
Matthew, D. (1983) *Atlas of Medieval Europe*, Oxford: Phaidon Press.
Muir, R. (1984) *History from the Air*, London: Michael Joseph.
Shea, M. (1981) *Maritime England*, London: Country Life.

Steinberg, S.H. and Evans, I. (1974) *Dictionary of British History*, London: Edward Arnold.

Treharne, R. and Fullard, M. (1973) *Muir's Historical Atlas*, London: George Philip.

See also publications by The Automobile Association (Drive Publications): e.g. *Treasures of Britain* (1968) and *Guide to Britain's Coast* (1984); and booklets published by Shire Publications, Cromwell House, Church Street, Princes Risborough, Buckinghamshire HP17 9AJ.

Appendix 3:
Some useful addresses

The Civic Trust
(Education Dept.),
17 Carlton House Terrace,
London SW1Y 5AW

The Countryside Commission
(Publications),
19–23 Albert Road,
Manchester M19 2EQ.

English Heritage
(Education Service),
15–17 Great Marlborough Street,
London WIV 1AF.

National Farmers' Union,
Information Division,
Agriculture House,
Knightsbridge,
London SW1.

The National Trust
(Education Office),
8 Church Street,
Lacock,
Chippenham,
Wiltshire SN15 2LG.

Tourist publications are obtainable through the regional tourist offices,
listed in Yellow Pages.

Index